BINGO
A Fresh Look at Grace

© 2015
Revised 2017

By Dr. Delron Shirley

Table of Contents

Delron Shirley
3210 Cathedral Spires Dr.
Colorado Springs, CO 80904
www.teachallnationsmission.com
teachallnations@msn.com

Bingo

A few summers ago, my wife's clan held a family reunion at the lake in northern Indiana where they grew up as children. For a full week in the late summer, a barrage of brothers, sisters, cousins, nieces, and nephews piled into a spacious waterfront lodge they had rented for the occasion. On one particular evening, we decided to entertain ourselves by playing Bingo; however, someone came up with some interesting alterations to the rules to make the game more engaging. We played one round by the traditional rules of getting a straight line, either horizontal or diagonal, across the board. After then, the procedure changed with each new match. One game required that the winner get "X"s in all four corners of his playing card. Another match required that the player get a perfect vertical row in order to win. Still other rounds called for such novel approaches as a total blackout of the card. We even played one round of "Last Man Standing" in which we all started by standing up and dropped out of the contest by sitting down when we actually scored "Bingo." In other words, the winner was actually what we would have always considered to be the loser since the person who won this round was the last contestant who hadn't scored a "Bingo" as all the others got what would have otherwise been considered a win. Yes, we were playing the same familiar game of Bingo, with the same familiar objective, and the same familiar general procedure; however, we needed a different, unfamiliar sequence of events in each new "hand" in order to score points. If you've never tried this variation of the game, I suggest that you do so someday – not for the sake of the game, but as a physiological experiment to see how it feels to sit at the table with what would normally be considered a winning card and not be able to stand up, wave your arms in the air, and shout "Bingo!" I can assure you that it is a totally uncanny feeling to lose when everything in your experience is telling you that you are a winner.

I shared this little narrative with you as a practical example of a powerful spiritual lesson about how we must learn to relate to God. But before I begin to apply this lesson to our daily lives, let me start with a bit of a history lesson – one that goes all the way back to the Garden of Eden. It's the study that theologians would call "Dispensational Theology," but let's not get hung up with terms. Instead, I'll just say that I want to look back at the Bible to see how God has dealt with the human race in different ways throughout history.

Most Bible scholars consider that the original period of the human family was called the Dispensation of Innocence because God created Adam and Eve with no consciousness of sin and without what we have come to call "original sin." Although we have no way of knowing how long the primal parents of the human race remained in this original state of innocence, biblical scholars generally consider that this dispensation covered a very short period of time. In fact, one scholar wrote that he calculated that it was less than one week since there is no mention of a second Sabbath day before the incident with the forbidden fruit. Although such an argument from silence is an extremely flawed exegetical approach, we can conclude from our general knowledge of the human species that it probably didn't take centuries, or even years, and maybe not even months, for Adam and Eve to start "testing their boundaries." At any rate, during this first dispensation – which began at Creation and ran until the Fall – there was one simple rule: don't violate your innocence. Of course, we are all too familiar with how this unassuming little regulation ended in utter failure as the serpent engaged Eve in a conversation that led to her violation of the rule about eating from the Tree of Knowledge of Good and Evil. The fate of the entire race was sealed when Adam took his wife's advice and followed suite by tasting the fruit of the tree.

This one act of rebellion hurled humanity into what Bible teachers call the Dispensation of Conscience in which man was expected to live according to his conscience. When we stop to look at the flow of events, it is easy to see that there is a very logical progression here. Adam and Eve lived in a world where they knew only good. In fact, the biblical record notes that, at the end of each day of Creation, God reviewed what He had made and determined that it was good. The only exception was that He felt that it was not good that Adam should be alone; however, once He created Eve, God proclaimed that it was very good. In this perfect world where there was not even a hint of evil, God gave our ancestral foreparents the simple test of having a chance to find out what evil was all about by tasting of the Tree of the Knowledge of Good and Evil. Once they ate of the forbidden fruit and obtained the knowledge of evil as well as the knowledge of good that they already had, God simply expected that they apply the contrasting information they now had and live according to the good they knew and had experienced while shunning the evil that they were now aware of. In other words, they were to live according their awakened consciences. At this point, it is interesting to note that the Living Bible actually translates the name of this tree as the Tree of Conscience. (Genesis 2:19) Unfortunately, man found it impossible to live by this simple rule of not violating his conscience, and this dispensation ended in failure when "God saw that the wickedness of man was great in the earth, and that every imagination of the thoughts of his heart was only evil continually." (Genesis 6:5)

As soon as man proved that he was incapable of following his conscience, God made the next logical step in His dealings with mankind. Although He had seen that the whole of humanity had perverted themselves into pursuing evil rather than good, there was one singular man – Noah – who caught God's attention because he remained a just and perfect man. (Genesis 6:9) With only one righteous man in the entire population, the most reasonable next step was to move into what has been labeled the Dispensation of Human Government in which the few – or sometimes one single – righteous individuals were to govern all the rest of the corrupted and imperfect population. The one simple rule of this dispensation was that the subjects were to not violate the leadership that God had put into place. Unfortunately, men could not follow this simple mandate. Almost as soon as they had come out of the ark, one of Noah's sons discovered his father unclothed in his tent and ridiculed him to the point that it attracted a curse upon all his descendants. In spite of this early failure, God allowed this flawed dispensation to stumble along until the time of Abraham.

At that point, He initiated a new dispensation, known as the Dispensation of Promise because it was based on the covenant promises that God spoke to His loyal servant Abraham. The covenant that God originated included a number of specific promises including the commitment to bless everyone who blessed Abraham and his seed while also cursing everyone who cursed Abraham or his seed. This promise was passed on through the generations until the time of the captivity in Egypt after the Jewish people immigrated there to escape the famine. It doesn't take a lot of creativity to imagine how the scenario must have played out. I can envision that several generations of Israelites continued to repeat the blessing of Abraham as they symbolically transferred the covenant from father to son. Yet somewhere along the line, one of the sons must have looked up to his aged father and scornfully demanded,

> What do you mean? "I'll curse those that curse you!" Everyday I'm cursed by the Egyptian taskmasters. Everyday, they whip and beat me. Everyday, they demand that I work like a dog for nothing. God never curses them. He hasn't made us blessed, and He hasn't given us this "Promised Land"! Why do you waste your breath reciting this old, dead tradition?

For four hundred years, the Israelites suffered slavery and persecution in Egypt. Their physical afflictions were tragic. But the real horror was in their loss of faith, hope, and vision. Exodus 2:24 states that God heard their groaning and that He remembered the covenant that He had made with Abraham. It was not the people who remembered that they had a promise and a blessing. The whole idea was lost to them. Only God remembered that to these people belonged a special covenant blessing. The whole foundation of the Dispensation of Promise had eroded away as the people failed to continue to believe what God had said to their forefather Abraham.

At that point, God took the next in the series of logical steps in His dealing with the human race by inaugurating the Dispensation of Law. The obvious logic was that since man could not follow his own conscience nor obey the human leaders that God would place in authority, the only reasonable remedy was to explicitly spell out everything that He expected of them. Therefore, God led them to Mt. Sinai where He gave them the all-inclusive Ten Commandments and all the explicit supporting regulations with one simple rule: don't violate the law. Unfortunately, the people – especially the religious leaders who were supposed to be the ones to set the example for the others – wasted no time finding ways to violate the intent of the law while appearing to observe the outward formalities of the regulations. That is, of course, except in the cases when they simply opted to blatantly rebel against the entire system of godly instruction.

At Calvary, God ended the Dispensation of the Law and introduced His ultimate plan of dealing with fallen humanity – the Dispensation of Grace. In this most magnificent move of divine intervention, God defied the whole system of logic that had characterized the step-by-step flow of the relationship of the Divine with His human subjects. In a mindboggling move that is just too much for our human logic and reason, God determined to take His own Son and make Him a substitute for all our human failures, frailties, and rebellion. By executing upon Jesus all the judgment that the human race deserved, God was able to look at humans as if they were no longer guilty or responsible for having violated the regulations of all the previous dispensations.

From biblical prophecies, we are able to understand that this dispensation will last until the Second Coming of Christ, at which point the final episode of the human-divine saga – the Dispensation of the Millennial Rule of Christ – will commence. In this culmination of the dispensations, Jesus Christ will physically occupy a throne in Jerusalem and personally rule the affairs of humankind.

Now, back to the Bingo game with my in-laws. It is important to remember that we were still playing Bingo, even if the rules for winning had been changed. At no point did the players put away the Bingo cards and take out the chessboard. Therefore, there was still a basic similarity that ran throughout the whole game. We still had squares to fill in, and the numbers were still distributed under the appropriate letters. Likewise, in the various dispensations of history, there are still basic similarities that overlap all the different eras, even if the final evaluation for salvation is counted differently. For example, Noah found grace in the eyes of the Lord even though he lived centuries before the Dispensation of Grace (Genesis 6:8), and believers today still must walk according to the leading of the Holy Spirit in their human spirits with a good conscience even though the Dispensation of Conscience ended millennia ago.

> There is therefore now no condemnation to them which are in Christ Jesus, who walk not after the flesh, but after the Spirit. (Romans 8:1)

I say the truth in Christ, I lie not, my conscience also bearing me witness in the Holy Ghost. (Romans 9:1)

This I say then, Walk in the Spirit, and ye shall not fulfil the lust of the flesh. (Galatians 5:16)

Now the end of the commandment is charity out of a pure heart, and of a good conscience, and of faith unfeigned. (I Timothy 1:5)

Holding faith, and a good conscience; which some having put away concerning faith have made shipwreck. (I Timothy 1:19)

Holding the mystery of the faith in a pure conscience. (I Timothy 3:9)

As I mentioned, this Bingo game was as much an experiment in human psychology as it was an evening of entertainment in that we had to learn to deal with our emotions as we would have to sit at the table with a "winner" that was actually a loser because the rules had changed. Imagine having a perfect "Bingo" but not being able to celebrate because this round of the game required that you have a vertical column or possibly all four corners filled. Well, that's just the same dilemma that humans always found themselves in spiritually as they moved from one dispensation to the next. Just when they figured out how to "play the game," the rules suddenly changed. Let's take just a couple examples to help us see what's going on. In the Dispensation of Innocence, Adam and Eve were naked. In all other dispensations, we are told to wear clothes. In the Dispensation of Conscience, people did what was right in their own eyes; however, this was sin in other dispensations. (Deuteronomy 12:8; Judges 17:6, 21:15; Proverbs 12:15, 21:2)

The most difficult transition of all seems to be the quantum leap that it took to move from the Dispensation of Law to the Dispensation of Grace. Even though we have been living in the new dispensation for two millennia, almost one hundred percent of Christians are still bound in one way or another to the rules of the bygone dispensation. We still want to do a good enough job of keeping the old rules in order to earn our salvation. We want to jump to our feet, flail our arms about, and yell out "Bingo!" when we get all the right spaces on our cards filled up, somehow ignoring that we're now playing by an entirely new set of rules. After all, why shouldn't we win when we have all the proper spaces ticked off?

> Under the "B," we have, "Belong to and attend church regularly."
> Under the "I," we have, "Inspirational literature, music, and movies are all I allow in my house."
> Under the "N," we have, "Never cheat on my wife or taxes."
> Under the "G," we have, "Give to the church and charities."
> Under the "O," we have, "Oppose all liberal political agendas (abortion, legalizing marijuana, same-sex marriages, etc.)."

Perhaps this transition is so hard because, as I have already mentioned, the move to grace is not logical. After all, all the religions of the world as well as all our secular relationships still operate by the "good enough" system. Additionally, we still read the Old Testament, which was written basically during the Dispensation of the Law. All the previous dispensations were wrapped up in a few chapters while the bulk of the thirty-nine books that make up the text convey the mentality of the Dispensation of the Law. Somehow it is just too difficult for us to understand that in the Dispensation of Grace we live by only laws that are repeated in New Testament and not by the ones that have been repealed.

Most Christians struggle – to one extent or another – with the question of how to balance the requirements of the Old Testament with the freedom of the New Testament. The struggle extends across the full spectrum from those who live every minute under an oppressive bondage to legalism to those who abandon all restraint in a devil-could-care attitude as they embrace freedom from the law yet still deal with that little voice that questions their illicit acts. I've seen the suffering that such struggles produce in the lives of believers – from the young man who became essentially a "basket case" as he would lock himself in his room for days on end repenting over his lack of being spiritual enough to the woman who essentially destroyed her life through alcohol trying to drown out the voice that warned her about her hedonism that she was sure was covered by God's grace.

The answer is actually clearly obvious in the scriptures. If something from the Old Testament has not specifically been negated in the New Testament – for example, blood sacrifice and dietary regulations – then it is still in effect. In fact, most of the Old Testament requirements are brought to even higher standards in the New Testament than in the Old Testament – for example, the New Testament's prohibition against lusting after a woman versus the Old Testament's commandment against the actual act of fornication. But as soon as we talk about the regulations, requirements, and obligations of the law, we must counter with the mercy, grace, and forgiveness of God. In the Old Testament, these qualities were demonstrated through the sacrifice system. But that system was incomplete in that it was only symbolic of the coming sacrifice that Jesus would make on Calvary. Therefore, the sacrifice had to be repeated after each violation of God's ordinances. In the New Testament, the sacrifice has been made once and for all; therefore, we don't have to repeat the sacrifice. We only have to acknowledge its effectiveness. Here is the freedom of the New Covenant – we follow God's rules with the knowledge that He has proactively dealt with our inability to totally fulfill them.

There are some game rules that remain constant throughout the game – the prohibition against murder, for instance. Murder was wrong when Caine killed Abel hundred of years before "Thou shalt not kill" was etched into the law. It is still wrong today, even though the Dispensation of the Law has been replaced by the Dispensation of Grace. These constants are often referred to as the moral laws of God, and the violations of these standards are classified as sins. The variables that come with each dispensation – especially the Dispensation of the Law – are temporary and apply only to those specific dispensations. An excellent example of this principle can be found in the transition period as the human race was accustoming itself to living under the law. When a man of the tribes of Israel was observed gathering sticks on the Sabbath, the people had no idea how to handle the situation. Ultimately there had to be an executive decision that he should be put to death for this infraction. (Numbers 15:32-36) Had he picked up sticks on the Sabbath the week before Moses ascended Mount Sinai, there would have been no problem; however, now that a new dispensation was in force, the people had to relearn the ground rules. As we transitioned out of the Dispensation of the Law into the Dispensation of Grace, Jesus had no problem directing the man that He healed beside the Pool of Bethesda to pick up his bed (an even bigger burden than the bundle of sticks that had resulted in the execution of the gentleman in the last example) and take it home on the Sabbath day. (John 5:1-10) The Jewish leaders, who couldn't understand that there was a new dimension dawning, had a major problem with this action because it violated the rules that they thought were still in place.

Let's revisit the reunion at that northern Indiana lake for just a minute. Remember that one of the rounds of Bingo was played by only trying to fill the four corners on the card. Since the corners appear under only the "B" and "O" columns, there was no need to call out the numbers that were picked from the "I," "N," or "G" categories. They simply didn't apply in this round. In like manner, we need to realize which categories of offenses are no longer applicable in each dispensation. Once we determine which rules do not apply, we need not even consider them. Theologically, the regulations of the law that were unique to that specific dispensation – including such things picking up sticks on the Sabbath – are known as ceremonial laws. These laws have no place in our current lives except as tutors to help us understand the overall plan of God that has been fulfilled in Christ. (Galatians 3:24)

We must learn to be careful not to try to live by the rules of a previous dispensation once the game has changed, else we will fool ourselves into believing that we're winners when we are totally losing the game. On the other hand, we could be totally winning and fail to realize it because we are still playing by antiquated rules that we aren't able to fulfill.

Under the "G" -- Grace

As we continue with our Bingo game, one call that seems to keep coming up repeatedly is the "grace" play. Let's take a minute to look at this little table of the number of times that the "grace box" was marked off in the various books of the New Testament:

Luke	1
John	3
Acts	10
Romans	20
I Corinthians	6
II Corinthians	13
Galatians	7
Ephesians	12
Philippians	3
Colossians	5
I Thessalonians	2
II Thessalonians	4
I Timothy	3
II Timothy	4
Titus	4
Philemon	2
Hebrews	7
James	2
I Peter	8
II Peter	2
II John	1
Jude	1
Revelation	2
TOTAL	122

There are two things that I hope you noticed from looking at this table. First, the term is significant in that it is used repeatedly in almost every book. However, there is one specific book – I Corinthians – that seems to have a disproportionately low number of references to this term. Compared to Romans, which is almost the same length, the Corinthian letter has less than one third the references. I think that there is a legitimate reason why the Holy Spirit deliberately directed Paul not to emphasize the doctrine of grace to this particular audience. The Corinthians were so carnal that Paul said he could not even address them as spiritual.

> And I, brethren, could not speak unto you as unto spiritual, but as unto carnal, even as unto babes in Christ...For ye are yet carnal: for whereas there is among you envying, and strife, and divisions, are ye not carnal, and walk as men? For while one saith, I am of Paul; and another, I am of Apollos; are ye not carnal? (verses 3:1, 3, 4).

Because he knew that the Corinthians would take the message and use it as an excuse to continue in their carnal conduct rather than as an opportunity to deal with their fleshly tendencies, Paul knew that he had to guard how he presented the message of God's grace to them. On the other hand, Paul so strongly stressed the doctrine of God's grace in the book of Romans that he felt it necessary to address the question that he knew would arise in the minds of his readers, "Can we continue to live in sin while under the blessing of grace?" (Romans 6:1) Apparently the apostle knew that the carnal Corinthians would immediately take advantage of the teaching without even stopping to ask the question and work through the implications. To the (hopefully) more mature believers he addressed in Rome, Paul wanted to make sure that he gave them a clear answer to the question about the possibility of continuing in sin as a result of God's open-handed forgiveness through His grace. In fact, the truth is that any time our teaching on grace does not open the door to this question, we have not taught grace to the same extent as did Paul. This question is the totally logical outcome when the new rules of this dispensation are explained explicitly.

In his response to this question, the apostle made it clear that our motive for living a holy life is not to earn credit. Holy living is a byproduct of our life in Christ, not a means for establishing it. It is the fruit – not the root – of our relationship with God. Our motivation for righteous living is because it is the outgrowth of our new nature and because it is a defense against the devil's inroads into our lives.

In order to properly understand what Paul was trying to communicate, we must first realize that forty-seven out of forty-nine times that the word "sin" is used in Romans, it refers to the nature of sin rather than to specific acts of sin. Therefore, Paul's emphasis is not on our actions – but on the power that sin has over the inner personality of humans. His point is that the specific acts of sin should no longer be an issue once this nature of sin is properly dealt with. Just as we can obviously sin without deliberately attempting to, we can – and should – also come to the place where we live righteously as part of our born-again nature. When this happens, we will actually live righteously without making an effort to do so and without trying to score points or earn merit through our good works.

Many believers are perplexed by the New Testament message of grace that they are totally free from Old Testament law. They wonder why we are still held responsible for the requirements of the Old Testament moral law if we are freed from the law through the grace of the New Testament. Perhaps the easiest way to comprehend this spiritual truth is to compare it to a physical reality. Most states have laws that require drivers and passengers in automobiles to wear seatbelts, drivers and passengers on motorcycles to wear helmets, and people in boats to wear (or, at least, to have available) life jackets. Such laws are actually nothing more than the reinforcing of common sense. Long before there was a specific legislation to enforce the practice of wearing a seatbelt, I made a conscientious habit of buckling up because it is the smart thing to do. The same is true with every requirement spelled out in the New Testament. Even if God in His grace will forgive us for violating the actual letter of the law, we are doing nothing but asking for trouble if we violate the spirit of the law. In other words, the New Testament requirements and regulations are a law of love in which God expresses His love for us by protecting us from the dangers that constantly lurk just outside the protective perimeters of these parameters. The scriptures make reference to those who know the truth yet live in unrighteousness.

> For therein is the righteousness of God
> revealed from faith to faith: as it is
> written, The just shall live by faith. For
> the wrath of God is revealed from heaven

against all ungodliness and unrighteousness of men, who hold the truth in unrighteousness. (Romans 1:17-18)

And with all deceivableness of unrighteousness in them that perish; because they received not the love of the truth, that they might be saved. And for this cause God shall send them strong delusion, that they should believe a lie: That they all might be damned who believed not the truth, but had pleasure in unrighteousness. (II Thessalonians 2:10-12)

Although some extreme proponents of the message of grace would claim that such people are examples of the gospel of grace in that God continues to love the sinner in spite of his sin, the scriptures clearly present individuals with such lifestyles as a disgrace to the gospel. Perhaps the whole discussion could be settled with one simple observation: the difference between the New and Old Testaments is the difference between grace and law – not grace and sin. God loves us even without our seatbelts; but He loves us enough to require that we use them. If we know the truth about the need to use a seatbelt but refuse to do so, we are in unrighteous rebellion and may be injured or killed – not because we broke a law, but because we disregarded His love.

The three great Christian qualities of love, faith, and grace are listed together in I Timothy 1:14, "And the grace of our Lord was exceeding abundant with faith and love which is in Christ Jesus. Therefore, as ye abound in every thing, in faith, and utterance, and knowledge, and in all diligence, and in your love to us, see that ye abound in this grace also." These three virtues are coupled together at least twice more in the New Testament (II Corinthians 8:7, Titus 3:15) and are seen as pairs in numerous other places in the scripture. Grace and love are companions in II Corinthians 13:14, Ephesians 6:24, and II John 1:3. Grace and faith are partners in Romans 1:5, 4:16, 5:2, 12:3, 12:6; II Corinthians 8:7; Ephesians 2:8; I Timothy 1:2, 1:14, 6:21; and Titus 1:4. Faith and love are positioned together in Galatians 5:6, 5:22; Ephesians 1:15, 3:17, 6:23; Colossians 1:4; I Thessalonians 1:3, 5:8; I Timothy 6:11; II Timothy 1:13; Philemon 1:5; and James 2:5. There is an obvious interdependence among all these qualities, but let's pick just three verses to see exactly how important their relationships to one another really are. Galatians 5:6 tells us that faith works through love. Second John 1:3 suggests that love is the foundation for grace in that truth and love are listed as prerequisites for grace, mercy, and peace. Romans 5:2 tells us that we have access to grace through faith. Therefore, we see that we don't have access to grace without faith, which is not effective without love, which is also a foundation for grace itself. In other words, the starting point for all Christian virtue is love. This love can motivate and activate faith that will manifest itself through the expression of grace. In our verse from the book of Timothy, we are able to see that none of this can happen outside of Jesus Christ. It is the life of Christ being lived inside of us that causes any demonstration of Christian virtues. In this we can finally understand why the scriptures are so adamant that it is not our works that produce salvation. It is His work through us that

19

demonstrates the salvation that He has given us!

In Romans 3:21-22, "But now the righteousness of God without the law is manifested, being witnessed by the law and the prophets; Even the righteousness of God which is by faith of Jesus Christ unto all and upon all them that believe: for there is no difference," Paul makes a clear distinction between righteousness and good deeds by stating that people can live by all the rules and regulations yet still be unrighteous in God's sight while those who don't follow all the obligations of the law can be seen as righteous in His evaluation. (Romans 2:26, 9:31, 10:5; Galatians 3:21; Philippians 3:6, 3:9) He then adds that it is possible to frustrate the grace of God by living as if we think that our righteousness is determined by our adherence to a set of rules and regulations. (Galatians 2:21) He goes on to give us a significant corrective by defining for us what it is that determines the righteousness that God accepts – righteousness that is birthed from faith and a life led by the Holy Spirit. (Romans 4:13, 10:4, 8:4) Good deeds that are motivated by our soulical or carnal nature or that are prompted by faith in our own ability rather than faith in God's work inside of us are ineffective.

The freedom that we find in grace is from the law, not from sin. By shifting the discussion – as does the question that Paul was addressing – from law to sin, we are missing the point just as Paul's audience did. To this misguided question, Paul's resounding answer is, "God forbid!" To get the full impact of how adamant Paul was in trying to communicate that we are totally off tract when we begin to think this way about his message of God's grace, let's check out some other possible translations of this interjection:

Heaven forbid! (Twentieth Century New Testament)
What a ghastly thought! (Philips Translation)
No indeed. (Montgomery's New Testament)
Let it not be! (Modern King James Version)
By no means! (Revised Standard Version)
Certainly not! (New King James Version)
Absolutely not! (Common English Bible)
Far be the thought. (Darby Translation)
May it never be! (World English Bible)
In no way. (Bible in Basic English)
Hell, no! (Cottonpatch Version)

Paul used this term eleven different times (eight times in the book of Romans alone) to describe his (and God's) adamant disapproval of the idea that Christians have a license to continue in sinful acts because God has extended His grace to them.

> God forbid: yea, let God be true, but every man a liar; as it is written, That thou mightest be justified in thy sayings, and mightest overcome when thou art judged. (Romans 3:4)
>
> God forbid: for then how shall God judge the world? (Romans 3:6)
>
> Do we then make void the law through faith? God forbid: yea, we establish the law. (Romans 3:31)
>
> What shall we say then? Shall we continue in sin, that grace may abound? God forbid. How shall we, that are dead to sin, live any longer therein? (Romans 6:1-2)
>
> For sin shall not have dominion over you: for ye are not under the law, but

under grace. What then? shall we sin, because we are not under the law, but under grace? God forbid. (Romans 6:15)

What shall we say then? Is the law sin? God forbid. Nay, I had not known sin, but by the law: for I had not known lust, except the law had said, Thou shalt not covet. (Romans 7:7)

Was then that which is good made death unto me? God forbid. But sin, that it might appear sin, working death in me by that which is good; that sin by the commandment might become exceeding sinful. (Romans 7:13)

What shall we say then? Is there unrighteousness with God? God forbid. (Romans 9:14)

Know ye not that your bodies are the members of Christ? shall I then take the members of Christ, and make them the members of an harlot? God forbid. (I Corinthians 6:15)

But if, while we seek to be justified by Christ, we ourselves also are found sinners, is therefore Christ the minister of sin? God forbid. (Galatians 2:17)

Is the law then against the promises of God? God forbid: for if there had been a law given which could have given life, verily righteousness should have been by the law. (Galatians 3:21)

One Bible teacher brought the whole discussion down to a very practical application by asking the same question in a very tangible way, "Would you commit adultery in order to learn how to appreciate your wife more?" Obviously not! If not, why should we feel that the fact that God has extended us grace from the law make us feel that we should take this grace as a license to sin?

According to Paul, the whole point of grace is to give us the authority and ability to live above sin – to, in his exact word, reign in righteousness.

> For if by one man's offence death reigned by one; much more they which receive abundance of grace and of the gift of righteousness shall reign in life by one, Jesus Christ. (Romans 5:17)
>
> That as sin hath reigned unto death, even so might grace reign through righteousness unto eternal life by Jesus Christ our Lord. (Romans 5:21)
>
> Knowing this, that our old man is crucified with him, that the body of sin might be destroyed, that henceforth we should not serve sin. (Romans 6:6)
>
> For he that is dead is freed from sin. (Romans 6:7)
>
> Let not sin therefore reign in your mortal body, that ye should obey it in the lusts thereof. (Romans 6:12)
>
> Neither yield ye your members as instruments of unrighteousness unto sin: but yield yourselves unto God, as those that are alive from the dead, and your members as instruments of righteousness unto God. (Romans 6:13)

For sin shall not have dominion over you: for ye are not under the law, but under grace. (Romans 6:14)

But God be thanked, that ye were the servants of sin, but ye have obeyed from the heart that form of doctrine which was delivered you. (Romans 6:17)

Being then made free from sin, ye became the servants of righteousness. (Romans 6:18)

For when ye were the servants of sin, ye were free from righteousness. (Romans 6:20)

But now being made free from sin, and become servants to God, ye have your fruit unto holiness, and the end everlasting life. (Romans 6:22)

For when we were in the flesh, the motions of sins, which were by the law, did work in our members to bring forth fruit unto death. (Romans 7:5)

But now we are delivered from the law, that being dead wherein we were held; that we should serve in newness of spirit, and not in the oldness of the letter. (Romans 7:6)

But sin, taking occasion by the commandment, wrought in me all manner of concupiscence. For without the law sin was dead. (Romans 7:8)

Wherefore the law is holy, and the commandment holy, and just, and good. (Romans 7:12)

Now then it is no more I that do it, but sin that dwelleth in me. (Romans 7:17)

For I delight in the law of God after the inward man. (Romans 7:22)

But I see another law in my members, warring against the law of my mind, and bringing me into captivity to the law of sin which is in my members. (Romans 7:23)

I thank God through Jesus Christ our Lord. So then with the mind I myself serve the law of God; but with the flesh the law of sin. (Romans 7:25)

For the law of the Spirit of life in Christ Jesus hath made me free from the law of sin and death. (Romans 8:2)

For what the law could not do, in that it was weak through the flesh, God sending his own Son in the likeness of sinful flesh, and for sin, condemned sin in the flesh. (Romans 8:3)

That the righteousness of the law might be fulfilled in us, who walk not after the flesh, but after the Spirit. (Romans 8:4)

Because the carnal mind is enmity against God: for it is not subject to the law of God, neither indeed can be. (Romans 8:7)

Wherefore? Because they sought it not by faith, but as it were by the works of the law. For they stumbled at that stumblingstone. (Romans 9:32)

For Christ is the end of the law for righteousness to every one that believeth. (Romans 10:4)

Grace, Foolishness, and Presumption

A number of years ago, Fredrick K. C. Price shook the charismatic church world with his book, <u>Faith, Foolishness, and Presumption</u> in which he challenged the readers to rethink what they were calling "faith." Through his common-sense approach to faith, Dr. Price was able to rescue a whole movement within the Body of Christ that was veering far off course in their zeal to live in faith. Perhaps it is time that we also ask ourselves if we can see the difference between grace and foolishness and presumption.

I'm certain that all of us have heard references to the difference between the God of the Old Testament and the God of the New Testament. To hear some teachers and preachers talk, you'd think that Jehovah had a total makeover during the intertestamental period. They present God as if He went into the dressing room as a judgmental legalist, ready to fling people into hell at any whim, and then came back out of the salon as a kinder, gentler deity who – like Santa in the Christmas parade – is indiscriminately tossing out goodies with no concern other than that the ones who grab up His treats express at least a cursory acknowledgement of His Son. There are many more errors in this theology than I can enumerate; however, let's tackle a few of the most glaring issues. First of all, God's nature and His Word are the only two consistent, immutable certainties in the universe. "That by two immutable things, in which it was impossible for God to lie, we might have a strong consolation, who have fled for refuge to lay hold upon the hope set before us." (Hebrews 6:18) He doesn't change. "For I am the LORD, I change not; therefore ye sons of Jacob are not consumed." (Malachi 3:6) He is the same yesterday, today, and forever. "Jesus Christ the same yesterday, and to day, and for ever." (Hebrews 13:8) There isn't even a hint of variation in Him, His purpose, or His nature. "Every good gift and every perfect gift is from above, and cometh down from the Father of lights, with whom is no variableness, neither shadow of turning." (James 1:17) Secondly, the Old Testament is just as much a book of grace as is the New. Certainly, the book is full of judgmental calls by the prophets, but the motivation behind each declaration was that the people were given a chance to repent and find the favor and grace that God was constantly extending to them. Thirdly, in the New Testament, God is no less holy than in the Old. He does not have any less strenuous standards for His people. He still condemns sin and sinfulness, warning us that such actions and attitudes will result in death and judgment.

> Know ye not, that to whom ye yield yourselves servants to obey, his servants ye are to whom ye obey; whether of sin unto death, or of obedience unto righteousness? (Romans 6:16)
> For the wages of sin is death; but the gift of God is eternal life through Jesus Christ our Lord. (Romans 6:23)
> Then when lust hath conceived, it bringeth forth sin: and sin, when it is finished, bringeth forth death. (James 1:15)

And whosoever was not found written in the book of life was cast into the lake of fire. (Revelation 20:15)
But the fearful, and unbelieving, and the abominable, and murderers, and whoremongers, and sorcerers, and idolaters, and all liars, shall have their part in the lake which burneth with fire and brimstone: which is the second death. (Revelation 21:8)

In chapter eight of the book of Hebrews there is a very significant quote from a "watershed" verse in the Old Testament that predicted the Dispensation of Grace that was to come in the New Testament, "Behold, the days come, saith the LORD, that I will make a new covenant with the house of Israel, and with the house of Judah." (Jeremiah 31:31) The promise of this new covenant is that it will be written in the hearts of believers. Under the old covenant, every intent of God had to be codified in the written law. That is why the Old Testament is so weighty compared to the relatively thin and concise New Testament. Under the law, there had to be a "chapter and verse" to refer to for even the most unlikely infraction. Under grace, we are given the indwelling Holy Spirit to direct our every thought, motive, and action. The other wonderful provision of the new covenant is that it provided for total forgiveness in which our sin would never be remembered again. The law never totally eliminated our guilt; it only offered appeasement for it. What a glorious provision we are able to receive in the Dispensation of Grace, but we must also remember that this glorious promise was given even in the Dispensation of the Law. But we'll never get the "punch line" of this verse unless we remember the context in which this verse originally appeared. The prophet had spent much of his book up to this point dealing with the rebelliousness of the people and the judgment that they are to experience as a result. In the verse leading up to this passage, he had just spoken about God's redemptive plan and said that the reason He had ploughed was so that He could plant and the reason He had torn down was so that He could build up. Next, the prophet unveiled the glory of God's restoration process – the new covenant that was to be established in the blood of Christ.

Even Paul, who was the champion of the gospel of God's grace toward sinful men, reiterated time and again that God's very nature prohibits the interpretation of grace that allows for men to willfully sin and not face consequences. What is new in the New Testament is not a new God but a new perspective in that we see salvation as a finished work rather than as a work in progress as in the Old Testament. Again, it is important to understand that God's graciousness was not a surprise in the New Testament; it was clearly foretold in the Old Testament. Let's consider, for example, Micah 7:9, "I will bear the indignation of the LORD, because I have sinned against him, until he plead my cause, and execute judgment for me: he will bring me forth to the light, and I shall behold his righteousness." This prophetic statement spoke of the shift from the Old Testament Dispensation of the Law to the New Testament Dispensation of Grace. It clearly testified of the human condition as man found himself continually under condemnation in his present dispensation because he could never live up to the requirements of the law. At the same time, it plainly predicted the Dispensation of Grace in which man's hope would be in the finished work of Jesus on the cross. Essentially, it described how Jesus "went to bat" in this period to plead the case for our justification.

Another intriguing Old Testament passage that foreshadowed the Dispensation of Grace is Zechariah 4:7, "Who art thou, O great mountain? before Zerubbabel thou shalt become a plain: and he shall bring forth the headstone thereof with shoutings, crying, Grace, grace unto you." The mention of the headstone in this passage is likely a prophetic reference to the coming of Christ, the messiah – the stone laid in Zion in Isaiah 28:16 and the rejected stone of Matthew 21:42. With this understanding, it is easy to see how the accompanying proclamation of a double dose of grace could be invoked.

> For the law was given by Moses, but grace and truth came by Jesus Christ. (John 1:17)
>
> Being justified freely by his grace through the redemption that is in Christ Jesus. (Romans 3:24)
>
> But not as the offence, so also is the free gift. For if through the offence of one many be dead, much more the grace of God, and the gift by grace, which is by one man, Jesus Christ, hath abounded unto many. (Romans 5:15)
>
> For if by one man's offence death reigned by one; much more they which receive abundance of grace and of the gift of righteousness shall reign in life by one,

Jesus Christ. (Romans 5:17)
That in the ages to come he might shew the exceeding riches of his grace in his kindness toward us through Christ Jesus. (Ephesians 2:7)
But unto every one of us is given grace according to the measure of the gift of Christ. (Ephesians 4:7)

If we don't get the full picture of what the Bible teaches about grace, it is easy to get a truncated view of the truth and to begin to perceive grace as a great cover to deal with our faults and errors. At that point, it is beneficial to consider an observation that someone once made about the way we can tell when grace is working in our lives. The explanation was that grace is effective when we don't panic if a need arises. This teacher followed up with the comment that falling from grace (Galatians 5:4) is when we start trusting in ourselves as our own means of salvation. The perspective presented in these two statements can help us to see grace as an actual trust in God's work in our lives rather than in our own ability to be good enough at keeping the rules. In other words, God's grace isn't so much about causing Him to ignore our shortcomings as it is about the power that works in us to give us the ability to live beyond such shortcomings. In fact, the whole reason that Jesus came to earth was to destroy the works of the devil in human beings. The proof that this work was accomplished is clearly visible in the victory that we can now have over sin.

He that committeth sin is of the devil; for the devil sinneth from the beginning. For this purpose the Son of God was manifested, that he might destroy the works of the devil. Whosoever is born of God doth not commit sin; for his seed remaineth in him: and he cannot sin, because he is born of God. (I John 3:8-9)

Notice carefully the wording of Paul's admonition to the Galatians, "I marvel that ye are so soon removed from him that called you into the grace of Christ unto another gospel." (verse 1:6)   His evaluation of the dilemma that the Galatians found themselves in was that they had moved away from Christ Himself. Yes, they had failed to maintain their relationship with the grace message, but the real issue was that they had actually abandoned Jesus. Later in the same book, Paul lamented the situation in this particular church, "Christ is become of no effect unto you, whosoever of you are justified by the law; ye are fallen from grace." (verse 5:4) Notice that he didn't say that their faith or the grace of God had become ineffective.   Their problem was that Christ Himself was no longer effective in their lives. Because they had become estranged from Christ, they were considered fallen from grace and His life was no longer effectual in them.

To understand this principle, let's take a look at what the Apostle James said about the operation of grace in our lives. In chapter four of his epistle, James referred to those who were involved in moral failures (adulterers and adulteresses), asking if they didn't understand that friendship with the world was enmity with God and that anyone who is a friend with the world is an enemy of God. (verse 4). He followed up in verse six with the assertion that in such cases God gives more grace, with the result in verse seven that they can then resist the devil.

> Ye adulterers and adulteresses, know ye not that the friendship of the world is enmity with God? whosoever therefore will be a friend of the world is the enemy of God. Do ye think that the scripture saith in vain, The spirit that dwelleth in us lusteth to envy? But he giveth more grace. Wherefore he saith, God resisteth the proud, but giveth grace unto the humble. Submit yourselves therefore to God. Resist the devil, and he will flee from you.

In two places in his short letter, James referred to the law of liberty (verses 1:25, 2:12), which seems to be an alternative description for grace in that it is the New Testament antithesis of the Old Testament law of obligation. In making reference to this law of liberty, the apostle said that some people just ignore it even when it points up their need and the opportunity God has given them to correct their shortcomings. He then continued with the statement that such people will be judged by this law of liberty. In other words, they will be held accountable for the fact that there was grace given them to deal with the faults in their lives but they didn't take advantage of that privilege and potential.

Grace is Sufficient

In II Corinthians 12:9, Paul shared a word of encouragement that he received directly from the Lord Himself, "My grace is sufficient for thee: for my strength is made perfect in weakness" – a message that apparently changed the apostle's whole approach to life. Prior to this word from the Lord, Paul had repeatedly asked the Lord to deal with his problems, but this one revelation revolutionized his attitude in that Paul now realized that there was a power residing inside himself that was adequate for dealing with his issues. He no longer anticipated that God would need to intervene in his circumstances; on the contrary, He had already placed a resident source inside the apostle that was sufficient for any situation.

From the context of the passage, we can understand that the grace that God had given the apostle – and all of us as well – is more than simply the unmerited favor that overlooks our human faults and frailty. From the wording of this prophetic message, it is apparent that the grace spoken of here must be seen as an actual strength – or at least a source of strength – rather than a merciful forgiveness for and a gracious excusing of our weaknesses. But before we explore that principle, let's take the time to examine the incident that was the catalyst behind this word from the Lord.

> And lest I should be exalted above measure through the abundance of the revelations, there was given to me a thorn in the flesh, the messenger of Satan

to buffet me, lest I should be exalted above measure. For this thing I besought the Lord thrice, that it might depart from me. And he said unto me, My grace is sufficient for thee: for my strength is made perfect in weakness. Most gladly therefore will I rather glory in my infirmities, that the power of Christ may rest upon me. (II Corinthians 12:7-9)

Although the Apostle Paul gave the explanation of his metaphor of the thorn in the flesh in the same line in which he mentioned this affliction, there has been a lot of confusion and controversy among those who would try to interpret the passage. When Paul speaks of his thorn in the flesh, many people get confused and fail to follow the logic that his problem was demonic. The difficulties are based on several misconceptions that people hold in their minds when they read the scripture.

The first difficulty arises from the word "exalted." Many Bible scholars assume that the apostle is saying that there was a danger that he might get too proud because of the revelations he had received – that he would become, as a mother might say of a little boy who was getting a little too cocky for his age, "too big for his britches." They think that Paul was suggesting that he might fall prey to the same trap about which he warned the Corinthians in his first letter: being puffed up through knowledge. (I Corinthians 8:1) In answer to this argument, we must remember that our heavenly Father is the giver of all good and perfect gifts (James 1:17), that He is a perfectly wise God (Romans 16:27, I Timothy 1:17, Jude 1:25), and that the blessings He gives us add no sorrow with them (Proverbs 10:22). Let's stop and think about things on a natural level for just a minute: would any wise parent who has the well-being of his child in mind give him a pocket knife before he learned the Boy Scout rules about how to hold the knife and the stick while whittling? If we, as humans, are smart enough to know how to pick age-appropriate gifts for our children and only give them gifts when they are old enough to handle them, isn't it much more true about our Heavenly Father who is perfect in wisdom. It would seem that there must be something else implied in the term "exalted" in this passage; however, we must first move to another issue before we can fully grasp what this word must be intended to communicate.

The second misconception centers on the source of Paul's thorn. Many scholars assume that it was God who put this thorn into Paul's life. However, we need to step back from the passage a bit and look at it in a broader scope to get a clear understanding. Consider the logic – or rather, lack of logic – in the assumption that God gave Paul this thorn. If God knows that the revelations He is giving Paul are possible sources for him to fall into error, certainly He would not correct the situation by inflicting some sort of difficulties. Although we do find many examples in the Old Testament of when God brought calamity upon His people as judgment and correction when they were in rebellion and idolatry, there is no biblical precedent for God's having put bad things in His people's lives as a preventative. God's pattern for preventing His people from going astray is through the written Word, His messengers such as prophets, and the personal direction of the Holy Ghost. Paul, as a mature believer and leader in the Body of Christ, would certainly have been able to hear and follow the voice of God without some sort of painful thorn being inflicted in his life. The whole idea that God placed the thorn in Paul's life is against the very nature of God as the giver of good gifts. It also contradicts the pattern by which He leads His children.

The next thing we must consider in determining the source of Paul's thorn is the text itself. Paul clearly told us that it was a messenger of Satan. Since it was Satan's messenger, why should we assume that it was sent by God? In order to answer this question, some Bible students have turned to a couple passages from the Old Testament (I Kings 22 and II Chronicles 18) where a lying spirit was sent to deceive King Ahab of Israel and King Jehoshaphat of Judah. However, careful examination of these incidents will reveal that these kings had already resisted the counsel and direction God had tried to give them; therefore, they – unlike Paul who was receiving and living by the revelations God had given him – were living in sin and rebellion. Furthermore, it must be noted that the lying spirit actually asked God's permission to go and deceive the kings. Therefore, it was not a case of God's having sent the evil spirit; rather, it was a case of His permitting it to go. A very similar scenario is played out in the life of King Saul in I Samuel 16:14. Since Paul's case does not parallel the cases of these rebellious kings of the Old Testament, we have no reason to try to equate the passages. The simplest way to interpret this passage is to read it as it is written – that Satan inflicted this thorn.

Having addressed the issue of the originator of the thorn, now we can go back the first question as to why it was sent. Seeing Satan as the originator of the thorn makes it readily obvious: it was sent to keep Paul from being exalted – or brought to a place of prominence in the church and world – because the Satanic kingdom suffered great losses every time Paul preached on the revelations he had been given. Even until today, the truths Paul brought to the Body of Christ are some of the most liberating principles ever taught. The devil desperately wanted to silence Paul. If he could keep people from receiving the apostle's message, he could keep them in his own clutches! This thorn was not God's way of protecting Paul from pride, but Satan's way of trying to prevent Paul from gaining a place of advantage in his assault against the kingdom of darkness.

One other thing to remember when contemplating Paul's thorn would be that Paul has specifically addressed the issue of those in the Body who begin to feel self-important and inflated. In Romans 12:3, he warned them not to think more highly of themselves than they ought to think. If, indeed, Paul knew that this sort of self-exaltation would result in receiving a thorn in the flesh, isn't it likely that he would have incorporated a warning about such a result in this admonition about our personal evaluations of ourselves?

The next issue to consider would be the determination of the exact nature of Paul's thorn. Many teachers have proposed the notion that it was actually an eye disease. They, of course, draw upon the fact that Paul was blinded for three days at the time of his conversion on the road to Damascus. Added to this is Galatians 4:15, "Where is then the blessedness ye spake of? for I bear you record, that, if it had been possible, ye would have plucked out your own eyes, and have given them to me," that they interpret to mean that he was having some sort of eye problem when he first preached in this city. In reality, Paul was using an expression similar to what we might use today by saying, "I'd give my right arm for you" – an expression which has nothing at all to do with anyone's need for an extra right arm but simply a way of expressing that you are so committed to a cause that you are willing to give something that is irreplaceable to help further that cause. The interpretation that Paul suffered from an eye disease ignores the fact that he was healed of the blindness when Ananias laid hands on him and the fact that the Galatians passage does not specifically mention eye disease or blindness. Any conclusions drawn from this verse are based totally upon inferences and implications, not on specific factual information.

However, we do have direct information and explanation concerning the nature of this thorn given in the text itself. Paul says that his thorn was a messenger from Satan. The English term "messenger" is translated from the Greek word *aggelos* that can also be translated "angel." Paul recognized that his thorn was one of Satan's angels (Matthew 25:41, Revelation 12:9) that we know as demons. His thorn was not a physical ailment at all, but a demonic attack upon his person in general and his ministry in specific. It was Satan's attempt to keep him from being established in a place "above measure," or above the capacity of the devil's forces. By simply reading the story of Paul's life, we can easily see that he was harassed on every side by zealous Jewish opponents who considered him a heretic and wanted to stop his evangelistic work, by jealous Christians who mistrusted him or thought that his acceptance of the gentiles without their having to abide by the Jewish law was in violation of the faith, and even by the tempestuous forces of nature. In a passage in the preceding chapter Paul spoke – as he does in the passage we are studying – of the infirmities in which he is determined to take glory. In this section, he gave a compilation of these obstacles that have been thrown across his path as he ventured out to advance the kingdom.

> Are they ministers of Christ? (I speak as a fool) I am more; in labours more abundant, in stripes above measure, in prisons more frequent, in deaths oft. Of the Jews five times received I forty stripes save one. Thrice was I beaten with rods, once was I stoned, thrice I suffered shipwreck, a night and a day I have been in the deep; In journeyings often, in perils of waters, in perils of robbers, in perils by mine own countrymen, in perils by the heathen, in perils in the city, in perils in the wilderness, in perils in the sea, in perils among false brethren; In weariness and painfulness, in watchings often, in hunger and thirst, in fastings often, in cold and nakedness. Beside those things that are without, that which cometh upon me daily, the care of all the churches. (II Corinthians 11:23-28)

This dark cloud that seemed to be following Paul around was actually a demonic force that manifested itself through various avenues – sometimes through the forces of nature, sometimes through the Jewish religious leaders, and sometimes even through Paul's Christian brothers.

When Paul asked the Lord to remove this demonic attack, the heavens were silent on his first two requests. On the third approach, Lord answered that the grace that Paul had already been given was sufficient for him to deal with the attack himself. God said that He didn't need to intervene because He had already made provision for Paul to deal with his adversary. Therefore, God Himself used the word "grace" to refer to a strength that was imparted to the apostle – and to all believers – that is potent enough to confront and defeat any attacker, whether natural, human, or demonic. In essence, God was saying that we must understand that grace is much more than His unconditional love and unmerited favor that overrides our faults and failures. God Himself was saying that grace is a force that is released in our lives powerfully enough to actually deal with and overcome the faults and failures that we too often use grace as an excuse to retain.

We have no indication as to when Paul had this encounter in which the Lord told him that His grace was sufficient. Perhaps it was in close coincidence with the Damascus Road experience, or perhaps it could have been years into his Christian life. In any case, it seems that Paul's realization that he could exercise the power of that grace had indeed empowered his life and ministry in that we see little or no evidence from Paul's writings that he was ever plagued by his shortcomings or the devil's accusations concerning them. One possible scenario could be that Paul was saying that the messenger from Satan was a guilty conscience over his weaknesses and that the grace that God had given him was the assurance that he was still okay regardless of all his past (and possibly continuing) failures. His greatest blunder would have been the fact that he at one time persecuted Christians and – according to Jesus' evaluation of the incidents – was persecuting Christ Himself. (Acts 9:4-5, 22:7-8, 26:14-15) The apostle does make several references to the fact that he was guilty of these atrocities:

> For I am the least of the apostles, that am not meet to be called an apostle, because I persecuted the church of God. (I Corinthians 15:9)
>
> Though I might also have confidence in the flesh. If any other man thinketh that he hath whereof he might trust in the flesh, I more…Concerning zeal, persecuting the church. (Philippians 3:4-6)
>
> Who was before a blasphemer, and a persecutor, and injurious: but I obtained mercy, because I did it ignorantly in unbelief. And the grace of our Lord was exceeding abundant with faith and love which is in Christ Jesus. This is a faithful saying, and worthy of all acceptation, that Christ Jesus came into the world to save sinners; of whom I am chief. (I Timothy 1:13-15)

Yes, Paul did confess his failures, but he immediately acknowledged that the grace of God was the more-than-sufficient remedy – not an excuse for him to continue in his disobedience, but a solution to not only the sin but also to the condemnation that resulted from it. Some might argue that Paul's statement that he was the least of the apostles because of his background as a persecutor was evidence that he was still under the condemnation of his past. However, we must read that statement in the context of all that Paul has said in this second letter to the Corinthian believers. In fact, he has already declared twice in the same letter that he was actually the very chiefest apostles (II Corinthians 11:5, 12:11) – the manifestation of the power of grace that caused him to overcome rather than to succumb to his human frailties, failures, and faults. Paul's conclusion is that because of the power of grace he could actually glory in (II Corinthians 12:9) and take pleasure in (II Corinthians 12:10) his weaknesses and failures because God's grace strengthened him to a point of victory and success. (I Corinthians 15:10, II Corinthians 2:14) His contemporary, the Apostle James, expressed this same point as being confident that when difficulties come God has a way to make sure that we come out on the other side perfect, entire, and wanting nothing. (James 1:4)

Now that we have mentioned the Apostle James, let's look at another of his statements in which he makes an interesting observation about grace, "But he giveth more grace." (James 4:6) How exactly can God give more grace? If grace is simply the unmerited favor and unconditional love that overlooks our faults and failures, then how can there be more of that? After all, once He has forgiven and forgotten our faults, what else is left for Him to give? Obviously there is more to giving more grace than simply pardoning our failures. Perhaps the answer to these questions is found in the gospel of John where the beloved disciple expressed that in Christ we have received grace for grace. (John 1:16) This passage has been rendered in a number of different ways in all the reliable translations – "grace for grace," "grace upon grace," "grace after grace," "grace because of His grace," "grace in place of grace," "grace on top of grace," and "grace over against grace." The difficulty in finding the right English wording stems from the fact that the preposition used here literally means: opposite, corresponding to, off-setting, over-against, in place of, what substitutes or serves as an equivalent for. Fitting any of these words into the context is difficult and confusing. How can grace offset itself or be opposite to itself, or serve as an equivalent for itself? Many Bible scholars have danced pedantically around the interpretation, giving little or no clarity to what the phase could mean. Some have suggested that the idea that John was trying to communicate was that the New Testament grace that is found in Christ (John 1:14) is a replacement for or the opposite of or the substitute for the grace expressed in the Old Testament. However, such an argument seems unfounded in that John makes the point in the very next verse that the Old Testament contrast to New Testament grace is law – not grace. Therefore, we need to continue an honest quest to determine how grace can become a replacement for grace – and, in doing so, it seems that the only way we can bring logic out of this seemingly illogical statement is to suggest that John is actually referring to two different kinds of or manifestations of grace – the grace that is the unconditional love and unmerited favor of God that pardons and refuses to hold our sins against us (Romans 4:8) versus the grace that gives us the strength to overcome temptations and sins (II Corinthians 12:9). If this is the case, then John was telling us that the fullness of grace that is found in Christ first gives us freedom from the condemnation of our faults and then moves into a second phase of actually giving us freedom from those faults themselves – a principle paralleled in Paul's counsel to his son in the faith, Titus, "For the grace of God that bringeth salvation hath appeared to all men, Teaching us that, denying ungodliness and worldly lusts, we should live soberly, righteously, and godly, in this present world." (Titus 2:11-12)

If this is the actual intent of John's statement that the fullness of Christ is received through grace upon grace or grace in place of grace, then we might expect that he would have fleshed the principle out in his gospel. And he did in the story of the woman caught in adultery. (John 8:3-11) I'm sure that we all know the story well enough that it is not necessary to repeat it here, but I do want to point out four specific movements within the story that relate to the opening passages in the gospel. The scribes and Pharisees brought the woman to Jesus asking Him to execute the penalties of Moses' law. Jesus answered by demanding that the sinless one among them should be the one to cast the first stone, and He then followed up by pardoning the lady. Here we see the exact elements of John 1:17 – the law versus grace and truth. The religious leaders wanted to enforce the law, but Jesus contrasted it by making them face the truth that they were not sinless and then extended grace to the woman. Here we see three movements – the Jews with a focus on the law, the self-examination that made them confront the truth, and the grace of God that allowed the woman to go free. But there is one other movement that makes the story complete – Jesus' parting words to the woman, "Go, and sin no more" –

the aspect of grace for grace or grace in place of grace of John 1:16. First Jesus offered the woman the grace to overlook her sin (I don't condemn you), but them He added the second dimension of grace to overcome her sin (Go and sin no more).

In this story, the condemned sinner experienced the same reality that the Apostle Paul later discovered – that God's grace is a strength sufficient to deal with any and every challenge that could possibly confront them. The same is true for us today!

Living in Grace

> But by the grace of God I am what I am:
> and his grace which was bestowed upon
> me was not in vain; but I laboured more
> abundantly than they all: yet not I, but
> the grace of God which was with me. (I
> Corinthians 15:10)

With a minimum of twenty-three specific references in the New Testament, the grace of God is a major theme in the Christian faith. (Luke 2:40; Acts 11:23, 13:43, 14:26, 15:40, 20:24, Romans 5:15, I Corinthians 1:4, 3:10, II Corinthians 1:12, 6:1, 8:1, 9:14, Galatians 2:21, Ephesians 3:2, 3:7, Colossians 1:6, Titus 2:11, Hebrews 2:9, 12:15, I Peter 4:10, 5:12) The concept consistently refers to the ability to live a life that is beyond what we could accomplish on our own. Although much contemporary teaching would interpret the idea to refer to God's unlimited forgiveness and unmerited favor toward unworthy subjects, the phrase consistently speaks of an ability placed within the believer so that he doesn't <u>have</u> <u>to</u> depend upon this undeserved forgiveness. Perhaps this is the same principle that Paul was referring to when he mentioned frustrating the grace of God. He explained that the reason the grace of God worked in his life was because he was no longer in control of his own life; rather, he had come to the place where he lived by the power of God within him.

> I am crucified with Christ: nevertheless I
> live; yet not I, but Christ liveth in me:
> and the life which I now live in the flesh
> I live by the faith of the Son of God, who

loved me, and gave himself for me. I do not frustrate the grace of God: for if righteousness come by the law, then Christ is dead in vain. (Galatians 2:20-21)

Earlier in this same chapter of Galatians, Paul told the story of a confrontation between himself and the Apostle Peter. A problem had arisen when Peter, who had been fellowshipping and eating with the gentile believers at Antioch, suddenly withdrew himself because a delegation of Jewish Christians from the mother church in Jerusalem showed up. Following his lead, other Christian leaders – including Barnabas, who had been instrumental in bringing the gospel to the gentiles – separated themselves from the non-Jewish brethren. More than the affront to the shunned brothers, Paul saw Peter's hypocrisy as an insult to the Lord and a contradiction to the message of the gospel. He used the occasion as a platform to present a powerful teaching on the transformation we have received through the grace of our Lord. In verse sixteen, he explained that no one is justified by his actions and that it is only by faith in Christ that we can be brought into right standing before God. He then added in the following verses that any action similar to Peter's attempt to live by Old Testament legalism once we have realized that we have been released from it would make us transgressors against the good work that God has done in our lives. He summed up our new position in Christ in the powerful wording of verse twenty where he stated that the essence of the Christian life to be fully crucified so that the life of God can manifest through us. He then concluded the discussion with as graphic terminology as possible to illustrate how offensive it is to try to earn our own merit. Such actions are actually a frustration of the grace that God is attempting to manifest in our lives.

In contrast to the possibility of frustrating the grace of God, Paul wrote to his protégé Timothy that he should "be strong in the grace that is in Christ Jesus." (II Timothy 2:1) When we look at this statement in the original Greek, we see that there is even more significance for the statement in that his wording actually said that Timothy should be strong <u>by means</u> of the grace that is in Christ Jesus. Unfortunately, many Christians use the grace of God as an excuse to be weak – saying that the grace of God will cover their failures – while quite the contrary is true about grace in that it is intended to make us able to overcome our propensity for failing. To get a grasp on what Paul was trying to communicate, let's refresh ourselves concerning Paul's explanation of the thorn in the flesh that he had to deal with. Paul's grasp of the grace of God determined whether he was to be doomed to endure this thorn or whether he could rise up and conquer it.

> And lest I should be exalted above measure through the abundance of the revelations, there was given to me a thorn in the flesh, the messenger of Satan to buffet me, lest I should be exalted above measure. For this thing I besought the Lord thrice, that it might depart from me. And he said unto me, My grace is sufficient for thee: for my strength is made perfect in weakness. Most gladly therefore will I rather glory in my infirmities, that the power of Christ may

rest upon me. (II Corinthians 12:7-9)

At this point, I don't want to take the time to dissect the passage fully. If you have questions concerning some of the conclusions I draw about this text, a full analysis can be found in my book <u>Finally, My Brethren</u>. In this present context, I simply want to make enough reference to the passage so as to establish an adequate setting for Paul's statement about the grace of God. Although many people assume that Paul's problem was medical, he made a clear statement that the issue with which he was dealing was a messenger of Satan. Thus, it was a demonic problem that could have manifested itself in any number of ways – physical, emotional, financial, social, spiritual, or through opposition or persecution by human agents. Regardless of the approach that the enemy used to attack Paul, the situation and solution were the same – Paul asked God to intervene, and God responded that He already had! God did not need to throw Himself into Paul's situation because He had already given the apostle the exact tool he needed to deal with whatever issues he was facing – His grace.

But before we look at that, let's take time to note just a couple observations that we can garner from studying the Greek background of the passage. The thorn in the flesh that Paul referred to here was literally a stake upon which decapitated heads were displayed. In other words, the devil was using the harassment that he was bringing against Paul as a trophy case to exhibit the seeming defeat of a Christian leader. Although this specific word isn't used in this particular passage, let's think about another name for Paul's adversary. The word "devil" means "one who throws through." This messenger from Satan was throwing accusations and lies totally through the apostle and penetrating him with them. But, praise God, Paul finally realized that he had the grace to deal with it! The Greek word for "sufficient" that God used when He reminded Paul of His grace literally means much more than what we might think at first. Essentially, it means "to be more than enough" or "to display abundance." In other words, Paul wasn't going to just barely crawl out of the ring with the devil. He was able to knock out his opponent! And so are we!!

Paul could have spent the rest of his life battling with this messenger of Satan had he not received the revelation that he already had the ability through God's grace to deal – once and for all – with his nemesis. The same principle is also true in our lives – revelation brings authority. The more we know about God, the more grace we can live in. For example: if we don't know that our God is a healer, we will not live in grace when the doctor says that we have some terrible disease. The more we know about God as our healer, the less disturbed we become when we get a negative report from the doctor. The fullness of grace is constantly with us, but we don't know how to appropriate it unless we know the One from whom it originates.

> But grow in grace, and in the knowledge
> of our Lord and Saviour Jesus Christ. To
> him be glory both now and for ever.
> Amen. (II Peter 3:18)

Before we go further into investigating what Peter has to say about the connection between the knowledge of God and grace, please allow me to make just one sidebar observation concerning this verse. There is a direct connection made in this passage between the grace of God and His glory. Grace is released so that glory can be revealed. This principle is developed even further in another of Peter's statements that we will study a little later, "his divine power hath given unto us all things that pertain unto life and godliness through the knowledge of him that hath called us to glory and virtue." Grace increases through our knowledge of God, and God's glory is manifested as grace increases. Unfortunately, many believers who have a truncated interpretation of God's grace that focuses only on His ability to forgive our shortcomings continue to live in failure and bondage to sin to the point that their lives prohibit the glory of God from being manifested. On the other hand, His glory can shine brightly through our lives when we grab hold of the power of grace to deal with all the messengers that Satan sends against us.

In Act 15:40 and several other instances when Paul or other Christian brothers were ready to embark on treacherous journeys where they could face natural disasters and human attacks, their fellow believers commended them to the grace of God. This act shows that grace is not the ability to sin and get away with it, but the ability of God to sustain you in every difficulty – temptations, tribulations, or persecutions.

Notice some of the powerful positive effects when grace is activated:

Grace provides all we need for godliness; it does not make an excuse for us to remain in ungodliness.

> Grace and peace be multiplied unto you
> through the knowledge of God, and of
> Jesus our Lord, According as his divine
> power hath given unto us all things that

pertain unto life and godliness, through the knowledge of him that hath called us to glory and virtue. (II Peter 1:2-3)

Grace ensures our inheritance in sanctification.

And now, brethren, I commend you to God, and to the word of his grace, which is able to build you up, and to give you an inheritance among all them which are sanctified. (Acts 20:32)

Grace leads us to obedience, not disobedience.

By whom we have received grace and apostleship, for obedience to the faith among all nations, for his name. (Romans 1:5)

Grace gives us the ability to stand, not fall back into carnality.

By whom also we have access by faith into this grace wherein we stand, and rejoice in hope of the glory of God. (Romans 5:2)

In the passage under consideration, Peter gave us an imperative and two avenues through which we are to accomplish this one command. He directed us to grow or mature in our Christian lives, and then he told us that the two arenas in which we are to grow are grace and the knowledge of Christ. The idea of maturing through knowing more about God and experiencing Him more intimately is a common theme in this chapter. (verses 2, 3, 5, 6, 8) Peter also mentioned the concept of maturing in grace in his first epistle when he spoke of achieving the end for the grace that is to be brought unto us at the revelation of Jesus Christ. (verse 1:13) With these thoughts in mind, we may need to rethink our understanding of grace as only the unmerited favor of God that redeems us from our sins. If this is the sum total of the definition of grace, then it would be impossible to grow in it, find an end to it, or see it multiplied. On the other hand, if we view grace as the ability that God gives us to deal with our ongoing struggle against the world, the flesh, and the devil, we can readily see how that it can be multiplied as we increase in our knowledge of Jesus. The more we understand about who He is and what He has accomplished in and for us, the more authority we can exert. (Ephesians 1:15-23) Likewise we can understand that the final step in this development will not come until we see Jesus in His fullness at His ultimate return. (I John 3:2-3) We simply will never be able to live in full grace unless we know everything about God.

> Grace and peace be multiplied unto you through the knowledge of God, and of Jesus our Lord, According as his divine power hath given unto us all things that pertain unto life and godliness, through the knowledge of him that hath called us to glory and virtue: Whereby are given unto us exceeding great and precious promises: that by these ye might be partakers of the divine nature, having escaped the corruption that is in the world through lust...For if these things be in you, and abound, they make you that ye shall neither be barren nor unfruitful in the knowledge of our Lord Jesus Christ. But he that lacketh these things is blind, and cannot see afar off,

and hath forgotten that he was purged
from his old sins...For if ye do these
things, ye shall never fall: For so an
entrance shall be ministered unto you
abundantly into the everlasting kingdom
of our Lord and Saviour Jesus Christ.
Wherefore I will not be negligent to put
you always in remembrance of these
things, though ye know them, and be
established in the present truth. (II Peter
2:2-12)

Notice that Peter spoke of the necessity of having
this knowledge of God to abound in our lives – not just
having a nonchalant or casual acquaintance with Him.
The Greek wording for the statement that grace
abounds speaks of a river overflowing its banks. Take
a minute to think about how much more clarity this
idea adds to the following verses:

Moreover the law entered, that the
offence might abound. But where sin
abounded, grace did much more abound.
(Romans 5:20)

Grace should be like a raging river flooding into our
lives any and every time sin tries to overtake us.

Therefore, as ye abound in every thing,
in faith, and utterance, and knowledge,
and in all diligence, and in your love to
us, see that ye abound in this grace also.
(II Corinthians 8:7)

In this context, Paul used the word "grace" to refer
to the spiritual ability to overcome human selfishness so
that we could become generous supporters of the
ministry. Paul's prayer was that the believers be literally

inundated with this godly power. The result would be that our generosity wouldn't just be a trickle, but a torrent or a gully washer, or perhaps even a tsunami!

> And God is able to make all grace abound toward you; that ye, always having all sufficiency in all things, may abound to every good work. (II Corinthians 9:8)

Wow! Did you grasp what Paul was saying in this verse? God is able to make grace so overflow in our lives that it will take care of every issue that we have to face. The result is that our lives will become like rivers at flood stage, flowing out of control with good works! This message is diametrically opposed to the erroneous interpretation of those who want to use "the grace card" as an excuse to continue in sin. "Grace" is not an I-don't-care attitude from God concerning our sin; rather, it is His intense love resulting in His willingness to forgive our failures – a love on God's part that should result in an intense love for Him on our part making us able to resist temptation. Chuck Swindol's comment on this truth goes something like this, "I need to learn the grace to refuse to use grace as an excuse for not refusing."

> For, brethren, ye have been called unto liberty; only use not liberty for an occasion to the flesh, but by love serve one another. (Galatians 5:13)

When we truly comprehend the principles and the power of grace, we will have such a flood of good works in our lives that there simply won't be any vacant room for the fleshly things that we would otherwise claim are "covered" by grace. Paul made a powerful observation in the book of II Thessalonians that can help us get a perspective on this truth.

> When he shall come to be glorified in his saints, and to be admired in all them that believe (because our testimony among you was believed) in that day. Wherefore also we pray always for you, that our God would count you worthy of this calling, and fulfil all the good pleasure of his goodness, and the work of faith with power: That the name of our Lord Jesus Christ may be glorified in you, and ye in him, according to the grace of our God and the Lord Jesus Christ. (II Thessalonians 1:10-12)

God's full intent for the Body of Christ is that He will be glorified in us. His objective is that our lives be such a magnificent manifestation of His presence that the world will stand in awe and reverence of the holiness and power that exudes from our very lives. Paul declared that he is continually praying that our lives would really match up to this divine expectation so that we can indeed be conduits of God's goodness and power to the world around us. He then added that all this would happen in accordance to the grace of God – meaning in direct proportion to His grace. Since His grace is unlimited, then the potential for this kind of divine life to be manifested in us is also unlimited. Someone commenting on this truth expressed his feeling this way, "Ones that others think aren't even worth the time of day are ones chosen by God."

Notice in his commentary that the key word in the hindering of our moving into the fulfillment of this high calling is that we think we are unworthy. That's why Paul also admonished us that we must renew our minds in order to begin to manifest the perfect will of God in our lives. (Romans 12:2) The Greek term for "sound mind" used in II Timothy 1:7, "For God hath not given us the spirit of fear; but of power, and of love, and of a sound mind," refers to a saved mind that is no longer affected by illogical, unfounded, or absurd thoughts – a blessing that most of us have failed to fully appropriate, keeping us from living in the true grace of God.

Paul gave us some powerful advice on how to develop a sound mind so that we do not continually wind up making serious mistakes and blunders. He wrote to the Galatians that if we could simply walk in the Spirit, we would not fulfill lust of the flesh. There is a world of difference between walking in the Spirit as opposed to trying to not walk in the flesh. In fact, this difference is the whole essence of the contrast between the Dispensation of the Law and the Dispensation of Grace. Under the law, we were required to make the physical effort to avoid certain actions and to make sure to fulfill certain other obligations. Under grace, we are required to allow the life of God within us to live through us so that we wind up living according to God's standards simply because of the new nature within us.

> This I say then, <u>Walk in the Spirit, and ye shall not fulfil the lust of the flesh</u>. For the flesh lusteth against the Spirit, and the Spirit against the flesh: and these are contrary the one to the other: so that ye cannot do the things that ye would. <u>But if ye be led of the Spirit, ye are not under the law</u>. Now the works of the flesh are

manifest, which are these; Adultery, fornication, uncleanness, lasciviousness, Idolatry, witchcraft, hatred, variance, emulations, wrath, strife, seditions, heresies, Envyings, murders, drunkenness, revellings, and such like: of the which I tell you before, as I have also told you in time past, that they which do such things shall not inherit the kingdom of God. But the fruit of the Spirit is love, joy, peace, longsuffering, gentleness, goodness, faith, Meekness, temperance: against such there is no law. <u>And they that are Christ's have crucified the flesh with the affections and lusts. If we live in the Spirit, let us also walk in the Spirit.</u> (Galatians 5:16-25)

I've emphasized a few lines in the paragraph to help draw attention to the point that Paul was trying to convey. His message that we are no longer under the law was not one that we should feel free to live in sin; rather, he was trying to teach us that in being free from the law we are free to live in the Spirit that produces righteousness. Let me give you a very practical example of how this difference works. Trying to avoid fulfilling fleshly lusts through our own willpower is like trying to <u>not</u> think about an apple. Now that I've mentioned it, I'll guarantee you that you can't erase the idea of an apple out of your mind. The only way to stop thinking about an apple is to begin to imagine an orange. Under the regulations of the law our focus will be on the rule about not thinking of an apple – with the "Catch 22" result that we have to constantly keep the "apple" concept in our minds so that we can avoid thinking about it. Under grace, we are given the sound mind that is now focused on an orange and, therefore, has no room for meditating on an apple. This is the power of God's grace versus the power of the law. Grace actually frees us from the fault while law brings us into continual bondage to the possibility of the fault. Grace not only frees us <u>from</u> the bondage of the law, it also frees us <u>to</u> follow the Spirit of godliness. In all reality, the fact that we are freed <u>to</u> produce the fruit of righteousness is actually more powerful than the fact that we are freed <u>from</u> the requirements of the law. Again, we have to realize that we are in an entirely new round of the Bingo game. If we don't renew our minds to the new rules of this particular round, we'll be yelling out "Bingo" when we actually have a losing card or – just as likely – trying really hard to fill in some spaces on our card that we don't need in order to score.

Confidence in Grace

In Ephesians 4:30, the Apostle Paul warned us that we should be careful not to grieve the Holy Spirit by which we are sealed unto the day of redemption. In this teaching, he addressed the significance of allowing the Holy Spirit to do His work in our lives. The Holy Spirit has sealed us as a result of our salvation, but it is ultimately important that we do not bring this security under question because of our disregard for His guidance that leads us away from the works of the flesh. In chapter six of the same book of Ephesians, Paul described the armor of God. He described one element of this protective gear as the breastplate of righteousness. (verse 14) Let's take a minute to consider the possible implications of looking at these two truths in light of one another. First, let's think of our own personal experience each time we do something that we believe to be wrong or fail to do something that we know that we should do. There is always an uneasy feeling in the core of our being – right in the center of our chests. The breastplate is the protective gear that protects that exact part of our being. Paul's description of this particular piece of armor is that it is righteousness, suggesting that righteousness actually protects that part of our personality that is affected when we err. Ultimately, it seems that Paul was telling us that there is a piece of armor that focuses on protecting our conscience. If this is, indeed, the message that he was trying to convey, it is easy to "connect the dots" and come to the conclusion that being careful to avoid grieving the Holy Spirit as He tries to guide us into righteous will give us a confidence that assures us through a clear conscience. On the other hand, we will lose this confidence if we disregard the Holy Spirit's promptings. By failing to maintain clear consciences, we open ourselves to accusations from the devil and a lack of confidence in ourselves, in our relationship with God, and in our ability to overcome the enemy. The New Testament clearly teaches that the power of a clear conscience is a major element in our lives and ministries.

> Paul, earnestly beholding the council, said, Men and brethren, I have lived in all good conscience before God until this day. (Acts 23:1)
>
> Herein do I exercise myself, to have always a conscience void of offence toward God, and toward men. (Acts 24:16)
>
> I say the truth in Christ, I lie not, my conscience also bearing me witness in the Holy Ghost. (Romans 9:1)
>
> For our rejoicing is this, the testimony of our conscience, that in simplicity and godly sincerity, not with fleshly wisdom, but by the grace of God, we have had our conversation in the world, and more abundantly to you-ward. (II Corinthians 1:12)
>
> Now the end of the commandment is charity out of a pure heart, and of a good conscience, and of faith unfeigned. (I Timothy 1:5)

Holding faith, and a good conscience; which some having put away concerning faith have made shipwreck. (I Timothy 1:19)

Holding the mystery of the faith in a pure conscience. (I Timothy 3:9)

I thank God, whom I serve from my forefathers with pure conscience, that without ceasing I have remembrance of thee in my prayers night and day. (II Timothy 1:3)

Pray for us: for we trust we have a good conscience, in all things willing to live honestly. (Hebrews 13:18)

Having a good conscience; that, whereas they speak evil of you, as of evildoers, they may be ashamed that falsely accuse your good conversation in Christ. (I Peter 3:16)

The like figure whereunto even baptism doth also now save us (not the putting away of the filth of the flesh, but the answer of a good conscience toward God,) by the resurrection of Jesus Christ. (I Peter 3:21)

Many Christians seem to have a faulty understanding of the work of conscience in the Christian life. Based on I John 3:20, "For if our heart condemn us, God is greater than our heart, and knoweth all things," and Jeremiah 17:9, "The heart is deceitful above all things, and desperately wicked: who can know it?" a teaching has spread through the church that God is bigger than our deceitful hearts and that we should not believe our hearts when we feel convicted or even condemned over our actions. After all, Romans 8:1 does tell us that there is no condemnation to those who are in Christ Jesus. The error with this teaching is that it stops short of the complete thought in the Romans passage by ignoring the fact that the promise of emancipation from condemnation is only promised to those who walk after the spirit rather than after the flesh.

The other problem is the confusion between the heart and the conscience. At various times in the scripture, the heart speaks of the soulical nature, the spiritual nature, and a combination of the soulical and spiritual natures of man. Conscience can also be seen as having a similar dichotomy in that it can be motivated by soulical stimuli (the culture we grew up in) or spiritual stimuli (the Holy Spirit). When Paul discussed the issue of eating meat sacrificed to idols, he spoke of the soulical conscience, saying that there was actually nothing wrong with eating the meat but there was still fault in the offence caused by violating our own consciences or in causing others to violate their inner feelings. (I Corinthians 8:7, 8:10; 8:12, 10:25, 10:27, 10:28 10:29) In other contexts, the scripture speaks of conscience motivated by our encounter with God, our spiritual conscience. (John 8:9; Acts 23:1, 24:16; Romans 2:15, 9:1; II Corinthians 1:12, 4:2; I Timothy 3:9; II Timothy 1:3; Titus 1:15; Hebrews 9:14, 10:22, 13:18; I Peter 2:19, 3:16, 3:21) In I Timothy 1:5, "Now the end of the commandment is charity out of a pure heart, and of a good conscience, and of faith unfeigned," we see that Paul understands the connection between the heart of man and our conscience, and we see that he is definitely speaking of the spiritual conscience in this context. Thus, the bottom line in what he is trying to say here is that if we ignore the messages that our consciences send to us we are in serious danger of making a disaster of our lives.

> This charge I commit unto thee, son Timothy, according to the prophecies which went before on thee, that thou by them mightest war a good warfare; Holding faith, and a good conscience; which some having put away concerning faith have made shipwreck. (I Timothy 1:18-19)

Some may challenge this idea by claiming that grace covers such blunders; however, we must remember that we have access to grace through faith. If we have made shipwreck of our faith by ignoring our conscience, how can we expect to ever make it to the port of grace? Although some may suggest that I John 3:20 (For if our heart condemn us, God is greater than our heart, and knoweth all things,) negates the conclusion I have just proposed, it is necessary to read the verse in its proper context. In fact, the very next verse actually affirms that there is a confidence that we can gain through a clean conscience.

> Beloved, if our heart condemn us not, then have we confidence toward God.

Allow me to share one anecdote from the life of Dr. Lester Sumrall to help answer those who may say that our consciences are not accurate indicators of God's dealing with us in that they are actually a reflection of what society has programmed us to think of as right and wrong. When ministering in the unreached jungles of South America, he was able to win a number of aboriginal women to Christ. After the meeting, they came to him and asked if he might be carrying an extra piece of cloth in his backpack. When he asked why they wanted his cloth, the women answered that they wanted to use it to cover their breasts. His response was that no one in the whole jungle where they lived wore anything above the waist and that he felt it strange that they wanted to do so. The women responded that they also didn't even understand their own desire but that they somehow felt uncomfortable ever since they had prayed with him. Proof positive that the Holy Spirit can and does overrule social influences! Certainly, there is a major aspect of social consciousness, but this does not negate the Holy Spirit's working in our hearts. If we want to have confidence in our grace lives, we must be careful to avoid grieving the Holy Spirit as He does His work of leading us into righteousness.

Closely paralleled with the concept of keeping a clean conscience is the doctrine of the fear of the Lord. Unfortunately, much of the teaching in the Body of Christ today minimizes or outright discredits this significant New Testament theme. It is easy to understand why we have shied away from this concept. After all, it is easy to misinterpret the idea with the result that we separate ourselves from God because we are scared of Him and begin to perceive Him as an angry God who is ready to punish us and send us to hell on a whim. However, in our attempt to avoid such as negative interpretation, we have swerved too far to the other side of the road to the point that the whole idea is in our "blind spot." Most of the teaching I have heard in the last number of years has denied that the fear of the Lord is a New Testament concept or has promoted the idea that any fear spoken of in this context should be translated as "respect." The problem with these two interpretations is that neither one is based on honest biblical research.

Those who hold to the idea that the fear of the Lord is restricted to the Old Testament simply haven't been reading their Bibles. There are more than a dozen direct references in the New Testament.

> Then had the churches rest throughout all Judaea and Galilee and Samaria, and were edified; and walking in the fear of the Lord, and in the comfort of the Holy Ghost, were multiplied. (Acts 9:31)
> A devout man, and one that feared God with all his house, which gave much alms to the people, and prayed to God alway. (Acts 10:2)
> Then Paul stood up, and beckoning with his hand said, Men of Israel, and ye that fear God, give audience. (Acts 13:16)
> And this was known to all the Jews and Greeks also dwelling at Ephesus; and fear fell on them all, and the name of the Lord Jesus was magnified. (Acts 19:17)
> There is no fear of God before their eyes. (Romans 3:18)
> Having therefore these promises, dearly beloved, let us cleanse ourselves from all filthiness of the flesh and spirit, perfecting holiness in the fear of God. (II Corinthians 7:1)
> Submitting yourselves one to another in the fear of God. (Ephesians 5:21)

Servants, obey in all things your masters according to the flesh; not with eyeservice, as menpleasers; but in singleness of heart, fearing God. (Colossians 3:22)

Honour all men. Love the brotherhood. Fear God. Honour the king. (I Peter 2:17)

But sanctify the Lord God in your hearts: and be ready always to give an answer to every man that asketh you a reason of the hope that is in you with meekness and fear. (I Peter 3:15)

Saying with a loud voice, Fear God, and give glory to him; for the hour of his judgment is come: and worship him that made heaven, and earth, and the sea, and the fountains of waters. (Revelation 14:7)

Who shall not fear thee, O Lord, and glorify thy name? for thou only art holy: for all nations shall come and worship before thee; for thy judgments are made manifest. (Revelation 15:4)

And a voice came out of the throne, saying, Praise our God, all ye his servants, and ye that fear him, both small and great. (Revelation 19:5)

Those who say that the fear of the Lord referred to in the New Testament is respect rather than fear haven't taken the time to look up the Greek wording of the texts. Each time the fear of the Lord is mentioned in the New Testament, the term *phobeo* is used. This is the same term that is used throughout the New Testament to speak of the kind of fear that we define as being "scared" or "terrorized."

Jesus and Paul both taught us concerning the coming wrath of God against the unrighteous (Matthew 3:7; Luke 3:7, 21:23; Romans 1:18, 2:5, 2:8, 9:22; Ephesians 2:3, 5:6; Colossians 3:6; I Thessalonians 2:16, 5:9); however, it is in the book of Revelation that we get the clarification that this term refers to a specific apocalyptic event rather than a general displeasure or anger on the part of the Almighty (verses 6:16, 6:17, 11:18, 14:10, 14:19, 15:1, 15:7, 16:1, 16:19, 19:15). If we miss the eschatological context of the term, we can wind up having a serious misunderstanding of the gospel and of the very nature of God. Many people live their lives in fear and dread of God, viewing Him as an angry judge who is continually looking for an occasion to punish His subjects. On the contrary, He is a loving father who is continually looking for an occasion to bless His children. We must certainly live our lives today being aware that there is a prophetic time when He will mete out His judgment. We must, therefore, accept His mercy and grace while it is available. However, once we have received His free offer of salvation, we need not dread or fear Him, thinking that He will unleash wrath upon us at any moment. Quite the opposite – He has delivered us from that coming day of wrath (Romans 4:15, 5:9; I Thessalonians 1:10) and has made a provision for us to come to Him for immediate forgiveness and eternal salvation.

> Let us therefore come boldly unto the throne of grace, that we may obtain mercy, and find grace to help in time of need. (Hebrews 4:16)

One other verse that we need to consider before leaving the topic of the fear of the Lord is Proverbs 16:6, "By mercy and truth iniquity is purged: and by the fear of the LORD men depart from evil." Notice that there are two distinct parts to the verse. The first has to do with the purging of iniquity (our inborn sinfulness), and the second has to do with departing from evil (the practice of committing sinful actions). The point of the verse is that there are two different remedies for the two different maladies. The sinful nature is dealt with through mercy and truth, but the sinful actions must be dealt with through the fear of the Lord. Here we see the delicate balance of grace and law. Grace (mercy and truth) takes care of the guilt of sin, but it takes the law or legalism (hating evil enough to fight against it) to eradicate sinful actions. Why should we ever be afraid of God? The answer is simple and direct, "Fear him which is able to destroy both soul and body in hell." (Matthew 10:28, Luke 12:5) If we are living in sin or have a propensity toward sinning, we genuinely need a healthy dose of the fear of God to keep us on the "straight and narrow."

> For if we sin wilfully after that we have received the knowledge of the truth, there remaineth no more sacrifice for sins, But a certain fearful looking for of judgment and fiery indignation, which shall devour the adversaries...It is a fearful thing to fall into the hands of the living God. (Hebrews 10:26-27, 31)

Of course we not only need to concern ourselves with the wrong actions that we might do (the sins of commission); we must also be aware of the good works that we need to make sure to fulfill so that we do not commit the "sin of omission." This aspect of the discussion brings us to the consideration of the place that works play in the Dispensation of Grace. One particular verse can serve to help us get a "bird's eye view" of some of the seemingly conflicting nuances of the topic.

> Also unto thee, O Lord, belongeth mercy: for thou renderest to every man according to his work. (Psalm 62:12)

Since the concepts of mercy and works both appear in the same verse, this one passage embodies both sides of a vigorous debate that exists in the church today. Many people in the Body of Christ are widely divided over the issue of how grace (or God's mercy) must be balanced against works. One "camp" holds tenaciously to the doctrine that God is not going to judge us in relationship to our works. They emphasize the point that verses like this one are from the Old Testament Dispensation of the Law while we live under the New Testament Dispensation of Grace today. They focus their understanding of our present relationship to God on many verses that say that our salvation is not according to our works.

> For the children being not yet born, neither having done any good or evil, that the purpose of God according to election might stand, not of works, but of him that calleth. (Romans 9:11)
> Where is boasting then? It is excluded. By what law? of works? Nay: but by the law of faith. (Romans 3:27)
> For if Abraham were justified by works,

he hath whereof to glory; but not before God. (Romans 4:2)

Now to him that worketh is the reward not reckoned of grace, but of debt. (Romans 4:4)

For if they which are of the law be heirs, faith is made void, and the promise made of none effect. (Romans 4:14)

Therefore it is of faith, that it might be by grace; to the end the promise might be sure to all the seed; not to that only which is of the law, but to that also which is of the faith of Abraham; who is the father of us all. (Romans 4:16)

And if by grace, then is it no more of works: otherwise grace is no more grace. But if it be of works, then is it no more grace: otherwise work is no more work. (Romans 11:6)

Knowing that a man is not justified by the works of the law, but by the faith of Jesus Christ, even we have believed in Jesus Christ, that we might be justified by the faith of Christ, and not by the works of the law: for by the works of the law shall no flesh be justified. (Galatians 2:16)

This only would I learn of you, Received ye the Spirit by the works of the law, or by the hearing of faith? (Galatians 3:2)

He therefore that ministereth to you the Spirit, and worketh miracles among you, doeth he it by the works of the law, or by the hearing of faith? (Galatians 3:5)

But that no man is justified by the law in the sight of God, it is evident: for, The just shall live by faith. (Galatians 3:11)

And the law is not of faith: but, The man that doeth them shall live in them. (Galatians 3:12)

Christ hath redeemed us from the curse of the law, being made a curse for us: for it is written, Cursed is every one that hangeth on a tree. (Galatians 3:13)

Not of works, lest any man should boast. (Ephesians 2:9)

Who hath saved us, and called us with an holy calling, not according to our works, but according to his own purpose and grace, which was given us in Christ Jesus before the world began. (II Timothy 1:9)

Not by works of righteousness which we have done, but according to his mercy he saved us, by the washing of regeneration, and renewing of the Holy Ghost. (Titus 3:5)

On the other hand, there are others who point to a number of other New Testament references indicating that God still judges believers according to their works.

For the Son of man shall come in the glory of his Father with his angels; and then he shall reward every man according to his works. (Matthew 16:27)

Therefore it is no great thing if his ministers also be transformed as the ministers of righteousness; whose end shall be according to their works. (II Corinthians 11:15)

That they do good, that they be rich in good works, ready to distribute, willing to communicate. (I Timothy 6:18)

That the man of God may be perfect, throughly furnished unto all good works. (II Timothy 3:17)

Alexander the coppersmith did me much evil: the Lord reward him according to his works. (II Timothy 4:14)

In all things shewing thyself a pattern of good works: in doctrine shewing uncorruptness, gravity, sincerity. (Titus 2:7)

Who gave himself for us, that he might redeem us from all iniquity, and purify unto himself a peculiar people, zealous of good works. (Titus 2:14)

This is a faithful saying, and these things I will that thou affirm constantly, that they which have believed in God might be careful to maintain good works. These things are good and profitable unto men. (Titus 3:8)

And let ours also learn to maintain good works for necessary uses, that they be not unfruitful. (Titus 3:14)

Therefore leaving the principles of the doctrine of Christ, let us go on unto perfection; not laying again the foundation of repentance from dead works, and of faith toward God.

(Hebrews 6:1)

And let us consider one another to provoke unto love and to good works. (Hebrews 10:24)

Of how much sorer punishment, suppose ye, shall he be thought worthy, who hath trodden under foot the Son of God, and hath counted the blood of the covenant, wherewith he was sanctified, an unholy thing, and hath done despite unto the Spirit of grace? (Hebrews 10:29)

Looking diligently lest any man fail of the grace of God; lest any root of bitterness springing up trouble you, and thereby many be defiled. (Hebrews 12:15)

What doth it profit, my brethren, though a man say he hath faith, and have not works? can faith save him? (James 2:14)

Even so faith, if it hath not works, is dead, being alone. (James 2:17)

Yea, a man may say, Thou hast faith, and I have works: shew me thy faith without thy works, and I will shew thee my faith by my works. (James 2:18)

But wilt thou know, O vain man, that faith without works is dead? (James 2:20)

Was not Abraham our father justified by works, when he had offered Isaac his son upon the altar? (James 2:21)

Seest thou how faith wrought with his works, and by works was faith made perfect? (James 2:22)

Ye see then how that by works a man is justified, and not by faith only. (James 2:24)

Likewise also was not Rahab the harlot justified by works, when she had received the messengers, and had sent them out another way? (James 2:25)

For as the body without the spirit is dead, so faith without works is dead also. (James 2:26)

And I will kill her children with death; and all the churches shall know that I am he which searcheth the reins and hearts: and I will give unto every one of you according to your works. (Revelation 2:23)

Reward her even as she rewarded you, and double unto her double according to her works: in the cup which she hath filled fill to her double. (Revelation 18:6)

And I saw the dead, small and great, stand before God; and the books were opened: and another book was opened, which is the book of life: and the dead were judged out of those things which were written in the books, according to their works. (Revelation 20:12)

And the sea gave up the dead which were in it; and death and hell delivered up the dead which were in them: and they were judged every man according to their works. (Revelation 20:13)

Before we go any further, it might be good to make one observation by referring back to our analogy of the Bingo game. If we ever feel that we can win the game through works, we have slipped back into playing the "blackout" round in which we needed to cover every single space on the board – a requirement that we have been freed from in this dispensation.

> For as many as are of the works of the law are under the curse: for it is written, Cursed is every one that continueth not in all things which are written in the book of the law to do them. (Galatians 3:10)

> For whosoever shall keep the whole law, and yet offend in one point, he is guilty of all. (James 2:10)

Let's consider two simple thoughts that may help clear up the issue. The first concept that I'd like to ponder is found in I Corinthians 3:11-15, which helps us to understand that God's judgment of believers is more of a judgment of our works than a judgment by our works.

> For other foundation can no man lay than that is laid, which is Jesus Christ. Now if any man build upon this foundation gold, silver, precious stones, wood, hay, stubble; Every man's work shall be made manifest: for the day shall declare it, because it shall be revealed by fire; and the fire shall try every man's work of what sort it is. If any man's work abide which he hath built thereupon, he shall receive a reward. If any man's work

shall be burned, he shall suffer loss: but he himself shall be saved; yet so as by fire.

The second concept comes from Ephesians 2:10, where Paul follows up his teaching on the fact that we are not saved by works by shifting the emphasis from our works to the work that God is doing in and through us. The significant point here is that it is not what we do for God but what we do through Him that counts.

For we are his workmanship, created in Christ Jesus unto good works, which God hath before ordained that we should walk in them.

Let's take a quick look at one other verse that can help us remember an important point that is often overlooked in the presentation of the gospel today.

Or despisest thou the riches of his goodness and forbearance and longsuffering; not knowing that the goodness of God leadeth thee to repentance? But after thy hardness and impenitent heart treasurest up unto thyself wrath against the day of wrath and revelation of the righteous judgment of God; Who will render to every man according to his deeds. (Romans 2:4-6)

As we stress the importance of the grace of God that provides salvation for us through faith without works, we often minimize the significance of righteous works and the necessity of forsaking unrighteous actions. In II Corinthians 6:1, Paul explained that works are still an important part of the life of the believer who has appropriated the true benefits of grace, "We then, as workers together with him, beseech you also that ye receive not the grace of God in vain." Even though he emphasized in other contexts this marvelous salvation through grace, Paul clearly stated that we will be held accountable for our actions and judged according to our deeds. He plainly taught that it is impossible to earn salvation by the deeds of the law (Romans 3:20, 3:28); however, he also clearly declared that we must take control of our actions and eliminate the ones that are birthed out of our corrupt carnal nature (Romans 8:13, Colossians 3:9). John reaffirmed this truth and even added that simply condoning others' evil deeds will bring us under judgment as accomplices to their evil. (III John 1:10, II John 1:11) Jude continued the discussion by declaring that judgment will be determined to individuals whose righteous deeds define them as righteous individuals and those whose unrighteous deeds define them as unrighteous. (verse 15) Jesus Himself, speaking in the book of Revelation, established the fact that He is observing our deeds as the determinate factor for His judgment. (verse 2:6, 2:22, 16:11)

We can never be saved by our deeds; however, our deeds are indicators as to whether God's grace has truly impacted our lives.

> Wherefore also we pray always for you, that our God would count you worthy of this calling, and fulfil all the good pleasure of his goodness, and the work of faith with power: That the name of our Lord Jesus Christ may be glorified in you, and ye in him, according to the grace of our God and the Lord Jesus Christ. (II Thessalonians 1:11-12)

This passage introduces a whole string of theological terms. If any one of them is misinterpreted or seen in the wrong light, the whole scripture becomes confused and confusing. First, let's look at the individual words; then we will see them all together; and finally, we will set the passage in its context.

"Count you worthy" doesn't have to do with our having to earn merit. It is God's decision as to what value He places upon us. Just as we say about physical property, "One man's trash is another man's treasure." Even when we may see ourselves as trash, He may see us as a treasure worthy of giving His very Son to redeem. "The good pleasure of His goodness" refers to His redemptive plan for our lives. Jeremiah 29:11 tells us that He knows the thoughts that He has toward us – thoughts of good, not of evil. Read in context, we see that God has good plans for His subjects even when they don't deserve His favor. "The work of faith" refers to the work that is done in our lives because we have faith. According to I John 5:4-5, this work will manifest in our ability to overcome the world. A victorious Christian life is not the result of our good deeds; rather, it is the product of really believing in the work that Christ has done inside of us. "Glorifying the name of the Lord," has to do with having a life that demonstrates the nature of God in the midst of a depraved and unregenerate world. (Matthew 5:16) "According to the grace of our God and the Lord Jesus Christ" tells us that the limitation of the effectiveness of all the other qualities the apostle is discussing is the amount of grace found in God and His Son. Of course, we know that He is totally full of grace (John 1:14) and that He has made that grace to abound unto us (Romans 5:17, 5:20; Colossians 1:12; I Peter 4:10).

Putting all these parts together, we can understand that this passage is a prayer that the work of salvation that God has determined toward us would prove effective in our lives. God has intended that His goodness would be demonstrated in our lives to the point that it would cause us to stand out in the sinful world that we inhabit and that the measure to which this would happen would be the very extent of His unbounded grace. Now, let's widen the scope and see what this statement says in light of the whole section.

As he opened this letter, Paul gave thanks that the faith, love, and patience of the believers were evident in the face of persecution and tribulation. He then added that such a demonstration of Christian virtue was a manifest token of the righteous judgment of God and that He will visit judgment on the persecutors while providing rest for the persecuted. The bottom line was that God expects that the work He has done in our lives should be evident and serve as a determinant factor in the sinful world.

Steps to Grace

I'm sure that we are all familiar with Jesus' statement about coming to Him and taking on His easy yoke and accepting His light burden; however, I'm sure that we can all find a refreshing new view of the passage by reading it from the <u>Message Bible</u>:

> Are you tired? Worn out? Burned out on religion? Come to me. Get away with me and you'll recover your life. I'll show you how to take a real rest. Walk with me and work with me – watch how I do it. Learn the unforced rhythms of grace. I won't lay anything heavy or ill-fitting on you. Keep company with me and you'll learn to live freely and lightly. (Matthew 11:28-30)

Wow! What a fresh perspective – unforced rhythms of grace. What intriguing, melodious words that seem to simply resonate and reverberate deep within the soul. What a powerful idea that grace has a rhythm – actually multiple rhythms. Perhaps we could liken the rhythm of grace to the waves of the ocean. If you've ever spent a lazy day just sunning by the seashore, you know the ultimately soothing – almost hypnotic – nature of the repetitive crashing of ocean waves as they break on the sands of the shore. Grace is the same – it continues to come in one surge or swell after the other. Perhaps we can liken the rhythm of grace to the sound of splashing water in a fountain or a waterfall. The spellbinding soothing sound of splashing water is universally recognized for its calming effect on the inner man. So powerful is that effect that parks, business offices, and even private homes incorporate fountains and water features into their design. Perhaps we can liken the rhythm of grace to the relaxing yet intriguing and haunting melodies of whales as these gentle giants of the deep communicate peacefully and serenely with each other. Whatever the melody of grace is, it is the song of peace within the human soul. As such, we must know how to, as the <u>Message Bible</u> says, rediscover life by finding our way to the rhythms of grace.

Guilt is the first step that can either lead us toward God or away from Him. We first have to realize that we are sinners who don't deserve God's forgiveness or mercy. If we turn that guilt into shame and turn away from God, we will fail to ever find His grace. However, if we respond with hope that He will pardon our sin, then we are on the road toward His grace. I believe that it was George Verner, founder of Operation Mobilization, who said, "Grace is the undeserved favor of God, and you are no candidate for grace unless you are undeserving. You can't be too down, too wrong, for grace. That's where Jesus gets His glory; not in the number of good Christians He pats on the back, but in the failures He restores." This is where grace begins.

Repentance is the next step that moves us away from our guilt and toward His grace. All the guilty feelings in the world will only keep us captive to our fallen state; however, a simple act of repentance breaks us free of the bondages of guilt and releases us to race down the highway of grace.

Acceptance is a major turning point on our journey to God's grace. Until we realize that He has accepted us

– regardless of our unworthiness – we will always live in condemnation and feelings of unworthiness. Remember the parable of the prodigal son? He felt guilt, and he repented; however, had he not come to receive the father's acceptance, he would have lived the rest of his life as a hired hand rather than the father's beloved son.

Confession is the next stride we must take toward the ultimate goal of experiencing God's presence. He wants us to confess the relationship we have with Him as a testimony before other men and all the hindering forces of the enemy. Vocally verbalizing our confession with our words releases the inner faith that we have in our hearts and gives us authority in our relationship with Him.

Eye contact is the final step to true grace. Just think of the natural dimension in which we avoid looking people directly in the eyes if we have guilt, shame, or unforgiveness in our hearts or if we feel that they are not accepting us. But when we have totally clear inner feelings toward others, we have no hesitance to look them directly in the eyes. So it is with God – when we have truly come to Him and experienced His grace, we have no hesitation to see Him face to face.

As we move toward grace, we will find that there are also certain things that we will move away from. Sometimes, we will discover that we have to make a deliberate attempt to rid our lives of these things; on other occasions, we will realize that these things have automatically fallen by the wayside as we have advanced in our relationship with the Lord. Let's look at a couple of these characteristics and then draw a conclusion from what we observe.

The first characteristic that I'd like to discuss is

selfishness. In order to explore this topic, let's compare what Paul wrote about Christian generosity with what some people say concerning the fact that grace has freed them from the obligations of the law of tithing and giving. Much of contemporary thought centers around the idea that tithing is part of the Old Testament law and that we are free from the curse of the Old Testament law. In just that short argument, there are several misconceptions and misinterpretations; however, I'd like to counter this argument with one simple thought to ponder: Maybe you want to be free from the curse of the law, but do you also want to be free from its blessing? The blessing of tithing is that it allows God to rebuke the devourer from your life. The real heart of the issue isn't how much or how little we give, it's the heart attitude in which we give it. Here is the dividing line between law and grace! If we have grace, we'll wind up giving way more than ten percent. That's why "grace" appears seven times in II Corinthians chapters eight and nine – the classic teaching on giving. In other words, Paul was saying to us that generosity is a manifestation of the fact that grace is operative in our lives. The converse would also be true: selfishness and stinginess are proof positive that grace has not had a real effect upon us.

In his first epistle, the Apostle Peter emphasized the second characteristic that I would like to consider: that pride and grace are contrary to one another, "Likewise, ye younger, submit yourselves unto the elder. Yea, all of you be subject one to another, and be clothed with humility: for God resisteth the proud, and giveth grace to the humble." (verse 5:5)

The topic is discussed even more thoroughly in James chapter four.

But he giveth more grace. Wherefore he saith, God resisteth the proud, but giveth grace unto the humble. Submit yourselves therefore to God. Resist the devil, and he will flee from you. Draw nigh to God, and he will draw nigh to you. Cleanse your hands, ye sinners; and purify your hearts, ye double minded. Be afflicted, and mourn, and weep: let your laughter be turned to mourning, and your joy to heaviness. Humble yourselves in the sight of the Lord, and he shall lift you up. (verses 6-10)

The conclusion that I'd like to draw from these two negative characteristics is that self-centeredness essentially hinders us from experiencing God's full grace. As we have already discussed, the basic approach to comprehending grace is defined by giving up the control of our own lives so that power of God can manifest itself within us. Paul summed it up in his letter to the Galatians:

I am crucified with Christ: nevertheless I live; yet not I, but Christ liveth in me: and the life which I now live in the flesh I live by the faith of the Son of God, who loved me, and gave himself for me. I do not frustrate the grace of God: for if righteousness come by the law, then Christ is dead in vain. (verses 2:20-21)

Pardon Me if I'm a Bit Hyper

I recently saw an otherwise sensible and respectable Christian television host attack what he called the "hyper grace movement" as the last deception that will deceive and destroy the end-time church. Although he was careful to avoid using names, his descriptions and quotes from the Bible teachers that he was referencing left very little room for doubt about what he was saying and which Christian leaders he was talking about. Incidentally, I happened to personally know some of the men he was talking about, and I can vouch for them that they are certainly not part of a movement to usher in the great delusion of II Thessalonians 2:10-12. As I watched this program, I felt a bit of a tingle of déjà vu from a few years ago when I heard so-called authorities accuse many of my fellow ministers as being guilty of teaching "hyper faith." In addition, I could even recollect the events of having personally been charged with being "hyper spiritual."

The "hyper spiritual" allegations came when, as a freshman in college, I joined a Christian fellowship group on the secular university campus where I was studying. I believe that I was the first person that most of these young believers had ever met who spoke in tongues. According to all their previous teaching, glossolalia was a tool of the devil that only manifested itself in demon-possessed individuals. Unknown to me, one of the other fellowship members who lived on the same hall in the dorm with me was assigned to spy on me to get proof that I was, indeed, the enemy's pawn so that they could expel me from the group before I infected them with any dangerous doctrine or demonic juju. Well, after six months of this secret surveillance, he gave his recognizance report to the overseers of the group. His conclusion was that he thought that I was a better Christian than anyone else in the fellowship.

The truth is that the entire history of the Christian church is riddled with the same story over and over again – just on different subjects. In Acts chapter eleven, we read the story of how Peter was essentially called on the carpet by the rest of the early church's leadership because he dared to enter a gentile's home and minister to him. He was "hyper liberal" as far as the rest of the church was concerned – a charge that continued to linger until Paul addressed it in Antioch. (Galatians 2:11-14) Paul was also subjected to an inquisition by the early church council in Acts chapter fifteen when they questioned his stance on allowing gentiles to become Christians without first becoming Jews and adopting all the religious trapping of the Old Testament faith. He was certainly "hyper tolerant" in his open-mindedness in their closed-minded society. Martin Luther was tried as a heretic because he was "hyper personal salvation." The Wesley brothers were stoned and pelted with rotten fruit because of their message of salvation that didn't require the religious regulations of the dominant church. I suppose that they must have been "hyper popular" in their approach to ministry. The early Pentecostals were mocked as "holly rollers," and their churches were burned. I remember hearing the story of one mob that attacked a Pentecostal church but felt that it would be wrong to burn a house of God; therefore, they ripped the building apart plank by plank and then ignited the pile of loose timbers. To these protestors, the Pentecostals were "hyper emotional" in their worship. Additionally, there were those Christians who were ridiculed as being "hyper healing" because they took an aggressive stand that God was able and willing to heal any and every disease. In the church, they were considered radicals; in the world they were seen as charlatans; and in some legal circles, they were even charged with practicing medicine without a license.

Once all the dust settled, all these "hyper" individuals wound up giving the Body of Christ something fresh, new, and revitalizing. Had it not been for "hyper liberal" Paul and "hyper tolerant" Peter, Christianity would be nothing more than a minor sect within the Jewish religion. Without the "hyper personal salvation" message of Martin Luther, we would still be trying to earn our salvation by climbing stairs on our knees and paying for indulgences. Had it not been for the "hyper popular" Wesleys, the Christian faith would be bound in traditional liturgy and ritualism. Without the "hyper emotional" Pentecostals, the modern church would minster to only our intellectual and social needs, neglecting the spiritual and emotional challenges and voids in our lives. The "hyper faith" movement awakened the Body of Christ as a whole to the reality of being able to boldly take new territory because we now know how to trust God in seemingly impossible situations. "Hyper healing" advocates ushered the church into a new level of intimacy necessary to overcome physical challenges and disabilities. Even my own "hyper spiritual" incident revolutionized the faith and prayer lives of countless students who went on to become significant Christian witnesses in their chosen secular fields.

The Bible clearly legitimizes the ministry of "hyper" prophets, evangelists, and worshipers. In II Corinthians 5:13, the Apostle Paul described himself as "being beside himself," a term that literally means outside of the control of his senses. In other words, he was "hyper spiritual" in his worship and ministry. Second Samuel chapter six records the story of how David danced so enthusiastically that it embarrassed his wife; yet, he determined to be even more "hyper emotional" in his praise. When Jesus began His ministry of preaching the gospel of the kingdom of God, healing the sick, and casting out devils, His friends came to restrain Him saying that He was beside Himself. (Mark 3:21) Need we even dare to mention the Prophet Isaiah who went around naked for three years? (Isaiah 20:2-3) If that's not "hyper," I can't imagine what would be!

It is my personal observation that it often takes a few people with tunnel vision to help the rest of us get a full view of what God has in store for all of us. Let me just invite you to sit back a little while and see how significantly the "hyper grace" teaching will mold the Body of Christ a little more into the true image of our Lord Jesus. If you would allow me to speculate for just a couple of minutes, I would like to suggest that one of the major influences that the current emphasis on grace will have in the Body of Christ will be a new revelation of the love of God toward His church. Although I've not done a scientific study and collected specific data on the topic, I have noticed a lot of popular songs that speak of the grace of God in the same manner that we might traditionally make reference to His love. Additionally, I followed in detail as one pastor who is a champion of the grace message shared his personal testimony of how he was released from his former religious bondage when he personally encountered the love of God. Although I had heard him share the same story many times in the past, the thing that kept me riveted to his testimony this time was that always before he had said that it was his revelation of God's grace that had set him free. But this time, he explained the same experience as an encounter with the love of God. Although there are some nuances that make grace and love different, a revelation of God's grace will certainly culminate in an experience of His love. And when that happens, we'll all want to raise our hands to heaven and shout "Bingo!" – or, at least, "Hallelujah!"

Back to the Original Game

Having said that we often need a few people with tunnel vision to help the rest of the Body of Christ get a full view of what God has in store for all of us, I want to make sure to clarify that we must be careful that our tunnel vision doesn't actually blind us to what we should be seeing because of others who are hyper about what God has shown them. I guess that the best way to explain what I'm trying to say here is to invite you into my classroom.

It was the last day of class before the final exam; so, as soon as I finished with the review, I opened the floor for any student questions. I always somewhat anticipate one of those "out in left field" questions when I do this, but I know the importance of giving the students an opportunity to ask for further insight into topics that might have been left a bit fuzzy in my teaching. And on this day, I did get one of those really "off the wall" queries when a student noted that I had taught at Dr. Lester Sumrall's college for many years and was now teaching in Andrew Wommack's school. She then commented that Lester Sumrall was essentially a "legend" in the "faith movement," while Andrew Wommack is seen almost as the "patriarch" of the "grace message." All that was the buildup to the bombshell she was ready to drop: "How did you transition from the faith to grace?" That question focused a brilliant spotlight on a major fallacy that has invaded the Body of Christ and, in many cases, crippled the saints.

The fact that there are different "camps" within the church is certainly undeniable. Such divisions date all the way back to the New Testament. In fact, the different persuasions over circumcision and the acceptance of gentiles who didn't observe the Jewish laws mandated the first church council in Acts chapter fifteen. The jealousy that arose between two different ethnic groups in the Jerusalem church occasioned the establishment of deacons to handle such internal affairs in Acts chapter six. And one of the initial issues that Paul had to specifically address in his letter to the church at Corinth was the matter of the theological divisions and personality cults that threatened the unity within the church. (Corinthians 1:10-13)

The divisions are just as – if not more so – marked today as they were in the first century. Actually, it is fairly common for believers to simply "write off" everything that is happening in the whole Body of Christ outside their little group, using the excuse that "they aren't preaching the gospel" simply because their emphasis may be on a different aspect of the faith. One graphic example occurred on the mission field when two teams decided to join forces to evangelize one specific community. Since one of the teams was not charismatic and the other one was, the resident missionary in the area asked that they focus totally on ministering salvation rather than trying to also lead the new converts in the baptism in the Holy Spirit. He explained to the charismatic group that he would do that in his follow-up sessions after the teams had gone back to America. However, one of the young girls felt that this was too serious a restriction to be imposed on her, and she became so angry that she verbally attacked the leader of the non-charismatic team – using a full array of four-letter words. To that situation, I could only say, "I guess that the fruit of the Spirit doesn't matter to you as long as you can have His gifts!"

But back the classroom; I started my response by quoting Ephesians 2:8, "For by grace are ye saved through faith," and commented that there was no division between the "faith movement" and the "grace message." I emphasized that it is impossible to obtain grace without faith; therefore, she would wind up with nothing if she tried to divide them. Had time permitted, I could have gone on with a number of other scriptures that demonstrate that grace cannot be appropriated without faith.

> Therefore it is of faith, that it might be by grace; to the end the promise might be sure to all the seed; not to that only which is of the law, but to that also which is of the faith of Abraham; who is the father of us all. (Romans 4:16)
>
> By whom also we have access by faith into this grace wherein we stand, and rejoice in hope of the glory of God. (Romans 5:2)
>
> And the grace of our Lord was exceeding abundant with faith and love which is in Christ Jesus. (I Timothy 1:14)

Actually, the whole question that she brought up can bring us right back to the Bingo board, but this time, let's think of the traditional way of playing the game – where you have to fill one square in each column and they have to be connected straight across, either horizontally or diagonally. Thinking of each column as representing a different emphasis of the Christian faith – a different "camp," if you will – we can see how that we will never win until we get rid of the disconnectedness and divisions within the Body of Christ. Starting with the verse that I quoted to the young lady on the left-hand end of the fourth row, we see that faith has to be connected to grace. Next, if we turn to Galatians 5:6, we'll see that faith is only activated by love, "For in Jesus Christ neither circumcision availeth any thing, nor uncircumcision; but faith which worketh by love." So, now we have another element that must be connected in order to appropriate grace. Of course, the next question would address how we can activate the love that makes faith work that allows us to obtain grace. The answer is in Romans 5:5, "And hope maketh not ashamed; because the love of God is shed abroad in our hearts by the Holy Ghost which is given unto us." This is the answer that the charismatics are ready to shout about – the Holy Spirit. But we're still not done until we ask about the source of the Holy Spirit. Jesus gave us that answer in John 15:26, "But when the Comforter is come, whom I will send unto you from the Father, even the Spirit of truth, which proceedeth from the Father, he shall testify of me." The Holy Spirit comes from Jesus and the Father – an answer that certainly makes the evangelicals happy.

When we put it all together, we see that it is impossible to score unless we all come into unity with the evangelicals talking about Jesus and the Father in their space under the "B," while the charismatics are covering the work of the Holy Spirit under the "I," and the humanitarians among us are camping out on the necessity for love under the "N." When we add the faith camp with their specialty under the "G" and the grace group with their specialty under the "O," we finally see that it is the whole Body of Christ compacted and fitly joined together with each member supplying his own special gift that makes us all winners! (Ephesians 4:16)

The church council in the fifteenth chapter of Acts is a great illustration of how grace works to bring all of the Body of Christ to a unity that benefits and blesses everyone. The whole thing started when men from Jerusalem (the center of the Jewish-oriented church where everyone basically followed the Old Testament rules and the Jewish traditions) showed up in Antioch (the headquarters of the gentile-oriented church where few of the members really understood the Old Testament regulations or Jewish customs and no one tried to live by them) and began to teach the gentile converts that they needed to adopt the same obligations that the believers in Jerusalem had imposed upon themselves. Apparently this was the first time that the grace versus legalism issue had "hit the fan," and – according to the biblical text – it was not a minor incident. The leadership in Antioch decided that the questions that were being raised were worthy of consideration by the very top apostles, so they sent Paul, Barnabas, and some other members from the Antioch church to Jerusalem as an official delegation to get "to the bottom of the matter." When Peter, James, and the other presiding spokesmen of the church weighed all the arguments and balanced them against the scriptures and the direction of the Holy Spirit, they made an official ruling: Christians were not obligated to live by the Old Testament regulations in order to be in good standing in the faith; however, there were certain courtesies that the Jewish-background believers asked of their gentile-background brethren. In essence, the Jews showed grace to the gentiles by acknowledging that they were Christians even though they were not circumcised. At the same time, the gentiles showed grace to the Jews by committing to abstain from eating meat that had been scarified idols, fornication, eating meat from animals that had been strangled, and from eating food that contained blood.

In the eighth chapter of his first epistle to the Christians at Corinth, Paul explained the theology behind the question of eating meat that didn't measure up to these standards. He concluded that consuming such meat was not wrong in and of itself; the believers had been freed from the regulations through grace. On the other hand, these same believers would be in error if their actions became offensive to another brother and caused a division within the Body of Christ; the grace on their lives required that they care more for others than for their own personal liberties. In other words, the grace of God worked two ways – in freeing the believers from the obligations of the law and in building unity in the Body of Christ by giving each member the authority to monitor his own actions for the good of the entire church family.

When these two aspects of grace function together, all the necessary pieces are finally drawn together and we have:

BINGO!!

Epilogue

The grace of the Lord Jesus Christ, and
the love of God, and the communion of
the Holy Ghost, be with you all. Amen.
(II Corinthians 13:14)

At least fifteen times, the New Testament writers offer the benediction that the grace of God would be with us. (Romans 16:20, 16:24; I Corinthians 16:23; II Corinthians 13:14; Galatians 6:18; Philippians 4:23; Colossians 4:18; I Thessalonians 5:28; II Thessalonians 3:18; II Timothy 4:22; Titus 3:15; Philemon 1:25; Hebrews 13:25; II John 1:3; Revelation 22:21) At first, we could assume that this was just a simple expression of blessing and not an actual theological statement. If we hold to the persuasion that every word of the Bible is inspired of God, we have to look a little deeper than to just assume that this phase is only a nicety.

If we do hold that there is an actual message in these words, we are faced with bit of a dilemma since we know that the grace of God is "standard equipment" with our salvation; it is not an optional add-on. However, the phrase doesn't imply that we don't have the grace of God; it specifically states that we would always have it <u>with</u> us. I keep a pouch of restaurant coupons in the glove compartment of my car, but occasionally my wife and I will decide to eat out when we are driving her car. In those cases, I have to pay full price for our meals because I do not have the coupons <u>with</u> me even though I <u>do</u> own them.

The apostles are praying that we will always have access to the grace of God – that unbelief, fear, or simply negligence not rob us of its wonderful benefits. May God's grace be with you always.

Books by Delron Shirley

Bingo, a Fresh Look at Grace
Christmas Thoughts
Cornerstones of Faith
Daily Bible Study Series (Five-Volume Set)
Daily Ditties from Delron's Desk (Five Volumes Available)
The Great Commission – Doable
Finally, My Brethren
Going Deeper in Jesus
In This Sign Conquer
Interface
Israel, Key to Human Destiny
Lessons Along the Way
Lessons from the Life of David
Living for the End Times
Maturing into the Full Stature of Jesus Christ
Maximum Impact
Of Kings and Prophets
Passion for the Harvest
People Who Make A Difference
Positioned for Blessing and Power
Problem People of the Bible
Seeds and Harvest
So, You Wanna be a Preacher
The IN Factors
The Last Enemy
Tread Marks
Verse for the Day (Two Volumes Available)
You'll be Darned to Heck if You Don't Believe in Gosh
Your Home Can Survive in the 21st Century

By Peggy Shirley

Women for the Harvest

Available at:
teachallnationsmission.com

CPSIA information can be obtained
at www.ICGtesting.com
Printed in the USA
FFOW05n0359191117

9 780990 557937